100 Cross-Stitch
Christmas Ornaments

100 CROSS-STITCH CHRISTMAS ORNAMENTS

Carol Siegel
and the

DIMENSIONS® DESIGN STUDIO

Meredith® Press
New York, New York

For Dimensions, Inc.

Editorial Director: Carol Siegel

Editorial Project Manager: Kristel Adair

Photographs: J. Edmund Lada

Produced by Dimensions, Inc.
For Meredith® Press

Director: Elizabeth P. Rice

Assistant: Ruth Weadock

Editorial Project Manager: Pat Van Note

Editorial Assistant: Carolyn Mitchell

Art and Design Advisor: Remo Cosentino

Production Manager: Bill Rose

ISBN: 0-696-02360-1

Library of Congress Catalog Card Number: 90-064238

Printed in the United States of America

10 9 8 7 6 5 4 3 2 1

All of us at Meredith® Press are dedicated to offering you,
our customer, the best books we can create. We are
particularly concerned that all of the instructions for
making projects are clear and accurate. Please address your
correspondence to: Customer Service Department,
Meredith® Press, Meredith Corporation, 150 East 52nd
Street, New York, NY 10022

Acknowledgments

Many talented people were involved in the labor of love that resulted in this book. From the designing and stitching of each of the 100 ornaments to the photography and writing, their enthusiastic efforts were geared toward one goal — that you enjoy every minute of creative stitching!

My very special thanks go to everyone involved in this project.

Carol Siegel

Carol Siegel

Art Direction:
Kristel Adair
Robin Beatty
Judy Connor
Elaine Cusatis

Photography:
J. Edmund Lada

Book Development:
Merry Babu
Tammy Barnhart
Nancy Bennecoff
Barbara Breton
Linda Dirkse
Barry Fogleman
Martha Freeman
Daniel Gorman
Sharon Gross
Cheryl Hatt
Terry Haupt
Margaret Hueske
Charlene Jamison
Elisabeth Ledig
Deborah Moyer
Pat Peifer
Magdalena Poch
Sue Roedder
Toni Schlitzer
Wendy Schuster
Brian Shellabear

Credits

Dimensions, Inc. would like to mention the following companies and individuals for their materials which were used in this book:

Redware Pottery in "A Primitive Country Christmas":
Ned Foltz Pottery
225 N. Peartown Road
Reinholds, PA 17569

Flatware in "A Merrie Olde Christmas"
Oneida Limited
Oneida, NY 13421

Fabrics:
Charles Craft
P.O. Box 1049
Laurinburg, NC 28352

Wichelt Imports, Inc.
R.R. 1
Stoddard, WI 54658

Zweigart / Joan Toggitt LTD
Weston Canal Plaza
2 Riverview Drive
Somerset, NJ 08873

Threads:
The DMC Corporation
107 Trumbell Street
Elizabeth, NJ 07206

Balger®
Kreinek
1708 Gihon Road
P.O. Box 1966
Parkersburg, WV 26012

Dear Cross-stitcher:

Each Christmas we revive old memories and create new ones. Family and friends gather around in fellowship to exchange gifts and share the joy of the season. We hope the projects in this book will become keepsakes of many happy Christmases.

Every family enjoys special rituals in the celebration of Christmas. The thrill to each of the senses is matched with the feeling of excitement and innocent wonder of a child, the beauties of nature, and the mystery of a starlit night. The 100 ornament designs presented here include a wide range of images that are a part of Christmas.

Everyone involved with this book is excited about the beautiful and inviting photography. We at Meredith are very proud of the many pages of full-color photographs, the clear instructions, and the number of projects that are here for our readers. We hope you'll use *100 Cross-Stitch Christmas Ornaments* for many years, and that the ornaments from this book will become part of your family's Christmas tradition.

Sincerely,

Pat Van Note

Pat Van Note
Editorial Project Manager

Contents

Preface

At no other time of the year are we so inspired to reach out to one another, to open our hearts and share, to rediscover the true meaning of love, as at Christmas. It is truly the most special season of the year, evoking feelings and memories that tickle all the senses....

> *...the scent of cinnamon and spice, balsam and mint, bayberry and pine*

> *...the taste of warm baked cookies, eggnog, pumpkin, turkey with sage dressing*

> *...the sound of a crackling wood fire in the hearth, a tinkling of bells, children's laughter, soft lullaby voices singing "Silent Night"*

> *...the vision of tiny white lights on a tree trimmed with red velvet ribbons, festive wrappings, garland twining down a banister, embroidered Christmas stockings, flickering candlelight dancing on delicate glass ornaments*

> *...the touch of prickly pine needles, the tender handling of each cherished ornament, a kiss under the mistletoe, a hug from a loved one*

> *...the feelings of anticipation and excitement, the joy of a child's innocence and wonder, the pleasure of sharing and remembering the traditions of youth*

At Christmas we create new memories with friends and family in the fellowship we share, the gifts we give, and the holiday treasures we create to celebrate the season. We would like to share some of our memories with you in this volume of counted cross-stitch ornaments.

Each chapter is devoted to a different theme in order to give you a variety of decorating styles. Finishing options are included in a separate chapter that enable you to choose the method you prefer. Each ornament includes instructions that make it easy for you to duplicate our original model, or change the colors, the fabric, or the finishing for a different look. The variations are countless.

We hope that this book will bring you many hours of stitching pleasure and happy memories in the years ahead as you welcome each Christmas season with these holiday keepsakes.

General Instructions

Fabric

The suggested fabrics for the ornaments in this book are Aida, Floba, various linens, and perforated paper. All fabrics are available in a variety of counts (number of squares or threads to the inch).

Aida — Evenly woven into small squares over which the cross-stitches are placed.

Davosa, Floba, Lugana — Evenly woven with coarse threads. Each cross-stitch is worked over a thread intersection.

Linen — Evenly woven with fine threads. Special techniques are used for stitching on linen. (See page 11).

Perforated Paper — Stiff paper evenly punched with holes.

To prevent your fabric from fraying, you can machine zigzag the edges, place tape over the edges, or apply a commercial non-fray liquid.

In order for the design to be properly positioned on the fabric for finishing, you will need to begin stitching at the center. You can find the center of a piece of fabric by folding it in half vertically, then horizontally. Mark the intersection of the folds with a pin or piece of thread. Use a ruler to find the center of a piece of perforated paper, marking it lightly with a pencil.

The center of the design chart can be found by following the arrows at the edges of the chart. If the chart does not have a stitch at the center, count to the nearest symbol, and begin at the corresponding point on the fabric.

We suggest that you stitch your design with the fabric held taut in an embroidery hoop. When you take a long break from stitching, remove the hoop to prevent it from marking the fabric. It is also a good idea to secure your needle at the fabric edge away from the design area to prevent a tarnished needle from marking your design.

If you stitch your design on perforated paper, you can hold the paper in your hand or carefully tack it to needlework stretcher bars to keep it flat. Care should be taken when stitching on perforated paper, since bending or excessive handling may damage the paper. If stitches are pulled too tightly, the paper will tear.

Embroidery Floss

All our designs were stitched with six-strand embroidery floss. The Anchor colors listed as replacements for DMC colors are only suggestions. They may not exactly match the colors originally chosen from the DMC collection. The best possible choice was made for each replacement, taking into consideration the other colors in the individual design.

To keep your floss from knotting as you stitch, cut the thread into short lengths, about 18" to 24".

Smooth, full-looking stitches are an attractive feature of counted cross-stitch. One technique to achieve this is to separate the length of floss into individual strands before threading the needle. Then, thread your needle with the number of strands you are going to use.

The thread can be easily separated by pulling out one strand at a time as shown.

Specialty Threads

Various specialty threads from Balger® were used on some of the ornaments. Japan Gold, Japan Silver, and red cord are metallic cords and are to be used by themselves. The other Balger® threads that were used are blending filaments. These fine filaments are to be threaded in the needle with the embroidery floss to give a lustrous effect.

Tips for Stitching

The chart below will help you to determine how many strands of floss and which size of needle to use on various fabric counts.

Fabric Count	Number of Strands	Needle Size
11	3	24T
14	2 or 3	24T
18	2	26T
22	1	26T

Always use an up-and-down motion to work your stitches, rather than a sewing motion. This enables you to work your stitches with an even tension and prevents your fabric from pulling out of shape.

If you use a hoop stand or if you lean your hoop against a table top, you can free both hands for stitching. This will greatly enhance your stitching speed. Keep one hand above the fabric and one hand below it. The top hand pushes the needle down through the fabric and the bottom hand pushes the needle back up through the fabric. If it feels awkward at first, try switching the placement of your hands.

Avoid using knots to anchor your stitching whenever possible. Knots will make your finished design look uneven, and they can work through the fabric. To anchor your first stitches, hold an inch of floss on the back of the fabric and secure it by working your first few stitches over it. To end the floss or to begin the next piece, run your thread vertically or horizontally through a few stitches on the back.

Try to avoid carrying your thread from one area to another, because it may show through the holes in the fabric on the front. It is better to end in that area and to start again in the new area.

If your thread becomes twisted as you stitch, drop the threaded needle from the fabric and it will unwind.

To correct misplaced stitches, gently pull them out with the needle, rather than cutting them out.

Always work your cross-stitches first, then add the details.

For each design, we have provided the dimensions of the stitched area in terms of the number of stitches. If you choose to work your design on a fabric with a different count than that which we used, the finished size in inches will change. You can determine the new finished size by dividing the number of stitches by the count of the alternate fabric. For example, a design which is 35 x 55 stitches would measure approximately 2½" x 4" on 14 count fabric and 2" x 3" on 18 count fabric.

$$35 \div 14 = 2\frac{1}{2}" \quad \text{and} \quad 55 \div 14 = 4"$$
$$35 \div 18 = 2" \quad \text{and} \quad 55 \div 18 = 3"$$

Tips for Linen Stitching

The slight variations in the weave and color of linen are normal features of this natural fabric and add to its charm and appeal. Linen is a versatile fabric in that cross-stitches can be worked over one thread, two threads, three threads or more.

For the linen designs in this book, each cross-stitch is worked over two threads as shown in the stitch diagrams. Thus, the count of linen fabric refers to the number of threads per inch, not the number of stitches. For example, 25 count linen yields 12½ stitches to the inch.

To give your cross-stitches proper support on the fabric, it is important that they be positioned correctly on the weave of the linen. The first half of each cross-stitch should be worked so that it starts and ends where a vertical fabric thread crosses over a horizontal thread as shown.

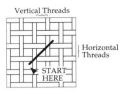

Design Charts

Each cross-stitch is represented on the design chart by a color symbol from the list of colors.

The details are also shown on the design chart and are given a written explanation. When Backstitch and Straight Stitch are listed together, use Straight Stitch for the single straight lines and Backstitch for all other lines.

Cleaning and Storage

If your design needs to be cleaned after you have finished stitching, please be aware that thread manufacturers have changed their thread dyes to make them biologically safer. As a result some colors such as red, red orange, dark blue, and black, which were once colorfast may now bleed when washed. To reduce the chance of colors bleeding and marking your work, we suggest the following cleaning method.

Because your design was worked with cotton embroidery floss, using a cold water wash intended for fine washables and wool garments may cause the thread to bleed. Instead, please use a mild dishwashing liquid and use lukewarm water to hand wash your embroidery. Rinse in lukewarm water until the water is clear.

Roll the embroidery in a towel and squeeze well to remove the excess water. Lay your embroidery flat to air dry. Don't press it dry with an iron.

If bleeding occurs, don't panic. Immediately soak your embroidery in lukewarm water. Change the water every two hours until the stains disappear.

To press your dry embroidery, lay it face down on a towel. Use a dry iron set to medium and press lightly so that you do not flatten the stitches.

Once you assemble your ornament, it is not feasible to clean it. To protect it from dirt and dust after the Christmas season, wrap it carefully in tissue and store it in a covered container.

Stitches

A FEW WORDS ABOUT THE DIAGRAMS: For all the stitches, the upper diagrams show the stitch worked on linen or Lugana. The lower diagrams show the stitch worked on Aida and should also be followed when working on Davosa, Floba or perforated paper.

Cross-stitch

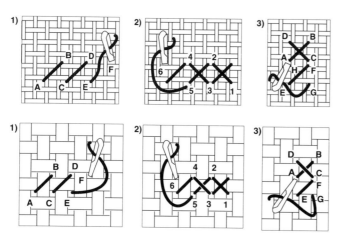

1 — Work across the row from left to right by coming up at A, going down at B, up at C, down at D, etc.

2 — Complete the other half of this row by working right to left. BE SURE THAT ALL STITCHES CROSS IN THE SAME DIRECTION. This is the key to beautiful cross-stitch.

3 — Work vertical stitches one at a time as shown.

Backstitch

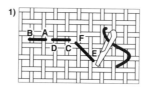
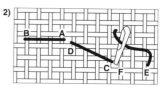
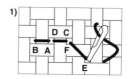
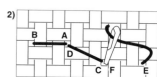

1 — Come up at A, go down at B. Come up at C, then go back down at D (same hole as A). Continue, always going back into the same hole as the previous stitch.

2 — Backstitches may be worked the length shown in diagram #1 or be irregular in length as shown in diagram #2. The method of working backstitches is up to you.

Straight Stitch

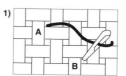

1 — Come up at A, go down at B, making each stitch the length of a line on the design chart.

Lazy Daisies

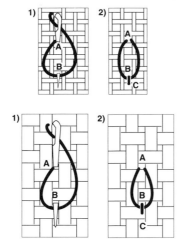

1 — Come up and go down at A, forming a loop. Come up at B, making your loop the size shown on the design chart. Make sure that the thread remains inside the loop as you draw flat.

2 — Go down at C to tack the loop in place.

French Knots

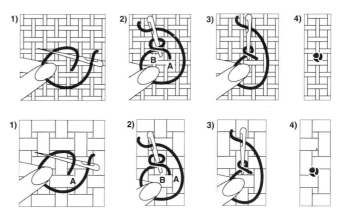

1 — Come up at A. Use one hand to hold the thread 2" away from A. Wrap the thread once around the needle.

2 — Continuing to hold the thread, insert the tip of the needle at B, right next to A.

3 — Pull the thread until the wrap is tight around the needle and lies next to the fabric. SLOWLY pull the needle through the fabric.

4 — Completed knot.

Smyrna Cross-stitch

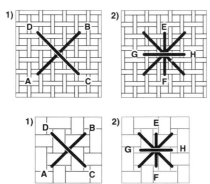

1 — Come up at A, go down at B, up at C, down at D.

2 — Complete the cross by working E-F, G-H.

Slip Stitch

1 — Work through a single layer of fabric. The broken lines show the path of the thread on the wrong side of the fabric.

A Primitive Country Christmas

Primitive and country bring to mind simple family pleasures. Cozy nights by a fire making decorations, gifts, cookies; spending time with family and friends. Old-fashioned, simple themes like folk art animals and toys, patchwork patterns and shapes. The sights of the season in colors and shapes to turn any house into a country home at Christmas.

Folk Art Angel

Finished Size: 4" x 2"
41 x 20 Stitches

SYMBOL	COLOR	DMC	ANCHOR
—	RED	321	47
—	DK. RED	498	20
—	GOLD	977	363
—	DK. GREEN	561	212
—	BLUE	311	148
—	TAN	738	372
—	SIENNA BROWN	433	358
—	DK. BROWN	3371	382
—	ECRU	Ecru	926

NOTE: The colors without symbols are not used for Cross-stitch; they are used for details only.

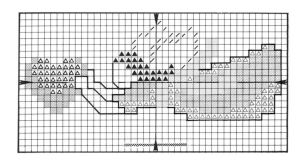

FABRIC: This ornament was stitched on 25 count brown raw linen. A 6" x 4" piece is needed. For stitching, hold the fabric with the long edges running horizontally.

CROSS-STITCH: Use three strands to stitch. Work each Cross-stitch over two fabric threads.

DETAILS: Use the number of strands indicated in parentheses.

Date — 561 (2) Backstitch: Use the numbers from
Personalizing Chart #8 (see page 155).
Pink lines — 433 (2) Backstitch
Black lines — 3371 (2) Backstitch

FINISHING: Our model was assembled using method #1, Cardboard Cut-Out (see page 156). Jute twine was used to trim the edges and to make a hanger and bow.

Holiday Steed

Finished Size: 4" x 2"
40 x 21 Stitches

SYMBOL		COLOR	DMC	ANCHOR
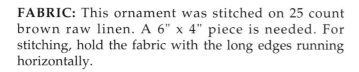	—	RED	321	47
	—	DK. RED	498	20
		MAROON	814	44
	—	GREEN	562	210
	—	BLUE	322	978
	—	DK. BLUE	312	979
	—	NAVY BLUE	823	152

NOTE: The color without a symbol is not used for Cross-stitch; it is used for details only.

FABRIC: This ornament was stitched on 25 count brown raw linen. A 6" x 4" piece is needed. For stitching, hold the fabric with the long edges running horizontally.

CROSS-STITCH: Use three strands to stitch. Work each Cross-stitch over two fabric threads.

DETAILS: Use the number of strands indicated in parentheses.

Black lines — 823 (2) Backstitch
Pink lines — 814 (2) Backstitch
Pink hearts — 321 (3) French Knots

FINISHING: Our model was assembled using method #1, Cardboard Cut-Out (see page 156). Jute twine was used to trim the edges and to make a hanger and bow.

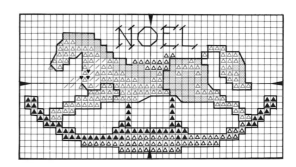

Mountain Santa

Finished Size: 2" x 4"
18 x 38 Stitches

SYMBOL	COLOR	DMC	ANCHOR
—	RED	321	47
—	DK. RED	498	20
—	PALE PEACH	754	4146
—	DK. GREEN	561	212
—	BLUE	311	148
—	NAVY BLUE	823	152
—	TAN	738	372
—	ECRU	Ecru	926

NOTE: The color without a symbol is not used for Cross-stitch; it is used for details only.

FABRIC: This ornament was stitched on 25 count brown raw linen. A 4" x 6" piece is needed. For stitching, hold the fabric with the long edges running vertically.

CROSS-STITCH: Use three strands to stitch. Work each Cross-stitch over two fabric threads.

DETAILS: Use the number of strands indicated in parentheses.

Tree branches — 561 (2) Backstitch

FINISHING: Our model was assembled using method #1, Cardboard Cut-Out (see page 156). Jute twine was used to trim the edges and to make a hanger and bow.

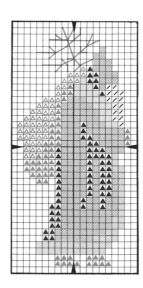

Pull Toy Sheep

Finished Size: 2½" Round
26 x 26 Stitches

SYMBOL	COLOR	DMC	ANCHOR
⟋⟋ —	RED	321	47
△△ —	BLUE GREEN	501	878
▲▲ —	DK. BROWN	3031	380
▦ —	ECRU	Ecru	926

FABRIC: This ornament was stitched on Zweigart 14 count oatmeal Rustico, color #54. A 6" x 6" piece is needed.

CROSS-STITCH: Use three strands to stitch.

DETAILS: Use the number of strands indicated in parentheses.

  Black lines — 3031 (2) Backstitch
  Black hearts — 3031 (3) French Knots

FINISHING: Our model was assembled using method #5, Wrapped Frame (see page 158). It was trimmed with a jute bow and hanger and ¾" wooden hearts.

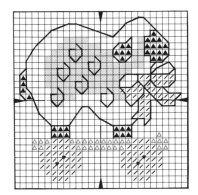

My Friend Sally

Finished Size: 2½" Round
25 x 26 Stitches

SYMBOL	COLOR	DMC	ANCHOR
⊡⊡ —	PINK	761	6
—	RED	321	47
▲▲ —	CRANBERRY	816	22
△△ —	BLUE GREEN	501	878
⊡⊡ —	LT. BLUE	931	922
▲▲ —	DK. BLUE	311	148
—	BROWN	3031	380

NOTE: The colors without symbols are not used for Cross-stitch; they are used for details only.

FABRIC: This ornament was stitched on Zweigart 14 count oatmeal Rustico, color #54. A 6" x 6" piece is needed.

CROSS-STITCH: Use three strands to stitch.

DETAILS: Use the number of strands indicated in parentheses.

Blue lines — 311 (2) Backstitch
Black lines — 3031 (2) Backstitch
Black hearts — 3031 (3) French Knots
Pink hearts — 321 (3) French Knots

FINISHING: Our model was assembled using method #5, Wrapped Frame (see page 158). It was trimmed with a jute bow and hanger and ¾" wooden hearts.

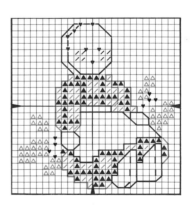

Christmas Goose

Finished Size: 2½" Round
22 x 27 Stitches

SYMBOL		COLOR	DMC	ANCHOR
▲▲	—	RED	321	47
△▲	—	GOLD	977	363
△△	—	LT. GREEN	502	876
▲▲	—	BLUE GREEN	501	878
		BROWN	3031	360
▦	—	ECRU	Ecru	926

NOTE: The color without a symbol is not used for Cross-stitch; it is used for details only.

FABRIC: This ornament was stitched on Zweigart 14 count oatmeal Rustico, color #54. A 5" x 5" piece is needed.

CROSS-STITCH: Use three strands to stitch.

DETAILS: Use the number of strands indicated in parentheses.

Black lines — 3031 (2) Backstitch
Black heart — 3031 (3) French Knot
Blue lines — 501 (2) Backstitch
Pink hearts — 321 (3) French Knots

FINISHING: Our model was assembled using method #5, Wrapped Frame (see page 158). It was trimmed with a jute bow and hanger and ¾" wood hearts.

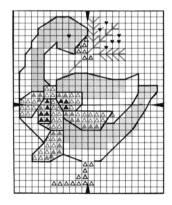

Patchwork Stocking

Finished Size: 2¾" x 3¾"
34 x 47 Stitches

SYMBOL	COLOR	DMC	ANCHOR
	RED	321	47
	FOREST GREEN	890	879
	DK. BROWN	3371	358
▨ —	ECRU	Ecru	926

NOTE: The colors without symbols are not used for Cross-stitch; they are used for details only.

FABRIC: This ornament was stitched on Zweigart red Lugana, color #906. A 5" x 6" piece is needed. For stitching, hold the fabric with the long edges running vertically.

CROSS-STITCH: Use three strands to stitch. Work each Cross-stitch over two fabric threads.

DETAILS: Use the number of strands indicated in parentheses.

Black lines — 890 (2) Backstitch
Blue lines — 3371 (2) Straight Stitch
Pink stars — 321 (3) French Knots

FINISHING: Our model was assembled using method #1, Cardboard Cut-Out (see page 156). The edges were trimmed with ⅛" piping. It was attached to the Patchwork Mitten ornament with a jute bow and string.

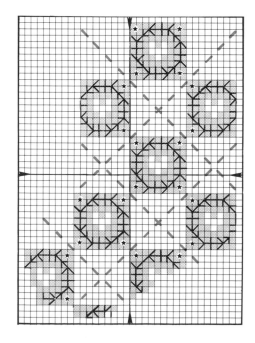

Patchwork Mitten

Finished Size: 2¾" x 3"
34 x 38 Stitches

SYMBOL	COLOR	DMC	ANCHOR
⊠⊠ —	MAROON	498	20
▦ —	LT. GREEN	320	215
	DEEP GREEN	500	683
▒ —	GRAY BROWN	840	379

NOTE: The color without a symbol is not used for Cross-stitch; it is used for details only.

FABRIC: This ornament was stitched on Zweigart brown Lugana, color #309. A 5" x 5" piece is needed.

CROSS-STITCH: Use three strands to stitch. Work each Cross-stitch over two fabric threads.

DETAILS: Use the number of strands indicated in parentheses.

Blue lines — 500 (2) Straight Stitch

FINISHING: Our model was assembled using method #1, Cardboard Cut-Out (see page 156). The edges were trimmed with ⅛" piping. It was attached to the Patchwork Stocking ornament with a jute bow and string.

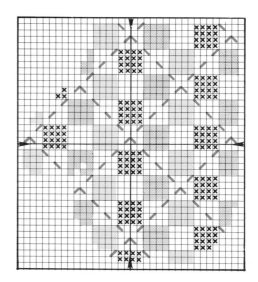

Snowflake Diamond

Finished Size: 4¼" x 4¼"
37 x 37 Stitches

SYMBOL	COLOR	DMC	ANCHOR
—	RED	321	47
×× —	GREEN	562	211
—	ECRU	Ecru	926

FABRIC: This ornament was stitched on Zweigart navy Lugana, color #589. A 5" x 5" piece is needed.

CROSS-STITCH: Use three strands to stitch. Work each Cross-stitch over two fabric threads.

DETAILS: Use the number of strands indicated in parentheses.

    Blue lines — 562 (2) Backstitch
    Black lines — Ecru (2) Straight Stitch

FINISHING: Our model was assembled using method #1, Cardboard Cut-Out (see page 156). The edges were trimmed with ⅛" piping. The stitched design was turned so it has a diamond shape and attached to the Folk Heart ornament with a jute bow and string.

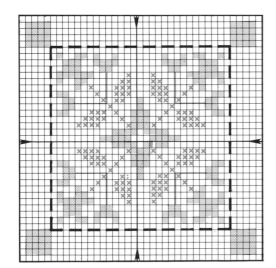

Folk Heart

Finished Size: 4" x 3½"
37 x 37 Stitches

SYMBOL	COLOR	DMC	ANCHOR
—	RED	321	47
—	GOLD	977	363
—	ECRU	Ecru	926

FABRIC: This ornament was stitched on Zweigart green Lugana, color #685. A 6" x 6" piece is needed.

CROSS-STITCH: Use three strands to stitch. Work each Cross-stitch over two fabric threads.

DETAILS: Use the number of strands indicated in parentheses.

Black lines — Ecru (3) Straight Stitch

FINISHING: Our model was assembled using method #1, Cardboard Cut-Out (see page 156). The edges were trimmed with ⅛" piping. The stitched design was turned so it has an upright heart shape and attached to the Snowflake Diamond ornament with a jute bow and string.

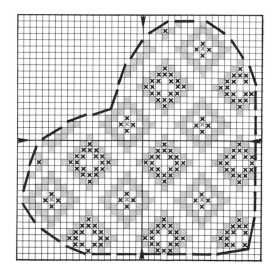

Here Comes Santa!

Santa Claus, Kriss Kringle, Père Noel, Father Christmas. Images of the figure that embodies the Christmas spirit are as different as the many cultures which have embraced this custom as their own. Whatever he looks like, his generosity, kindliness, and goodness represent the best of the Christmas season.

Jolly Santa

Finished Size: 3" Round
28 x 32 Stitches

SYMBOL	COLOR		DMC	ANCHOR
	—	PALE PEACH	754	4146
	—	PINK	894	26
	—	RED	666	46
	—	GREEN	700	229
	—	BLACK	310	403

FABRIC: This ornament was stitched on Zweigart 14 count white Aida. A 5" x 5" piece is needed.

CROSS-STITCH: Use three strands to stitch.

DETAILS: Use the number of strands indicated in parentheses.

Black lines — 310 (1) Backstitch
Pink hearts — 666 (6) French Knots

FINISHING: Our model was assembled using method #9, Ready-Made Frame (see page 159). A ½" pom-pom was glued to the tip of Santa's hat. The bow was tied with ⅛" satin ribbon and glued to the frame with faux holly leaves.

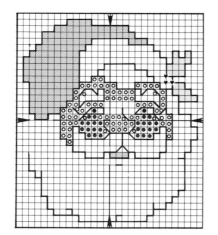

Primitive Santa

Finished Size: 2¼" x 4½"
25 x 56 Stitches

SYMBOL	COLOR	DMC	ANCHOR
—	PALE PEACH	754	4146
—	PINK	760	9
—	RED	321	47
—	DK. RED	498	44
—	GREEN	989	257
—	DK. GREEN	986	246
—	CREAM	739	366
—	TAN	738	367
—	LT. BROWN	301	351
—	DK. BROWN	3371	381
—	WHITE	White	1

FABRIC: This ornament was stitched on Zweigart 18 count Floba, color #53. A 5" x 9" piece is needed. For stitching, hold the fabric so the long sides run vertically.

CROSS-STITCH: Use two strands to stitch.

DETAILS: Use the number of strands indicated in parentheses.

   Thick black line — White (6) Straight Stitch
   Thin black lines — 3371 (1) Backstitch

FINISHING: Our model was assembled with natural wood hardware using method #2, Bellpull Banner (see page 157). The Monk's Cording hanger was made with twelve strands of DMC #321.

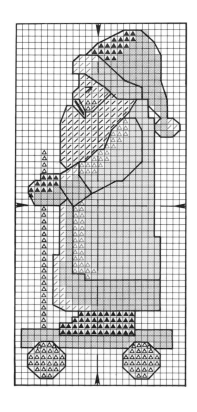

Father Christmas

Finished Size: 3" x 4"
36 x 60 Stitches

SYMBOL	COLOR	DMC	ANCHOR
J J	PALE PEACH	754	778
● ●	RED	321	9046
o o	GOLD	783	307
o o	GREEN	502	216
	DK. GREEN	501	218
x x	BLUE	322	978
● ●	DK. BLUE	312	979
x x	TAN	738	367
	DK. TAN	437	368
o o	LT. BROWN	434	370
	BROWN	433	371
	DK. BROWN	3031	360
● ●	BLACK	310	403
x x	CREAM	712	276

NOTE: *The color without a symbol is not used for Cross-stitch; it is used for details only.*

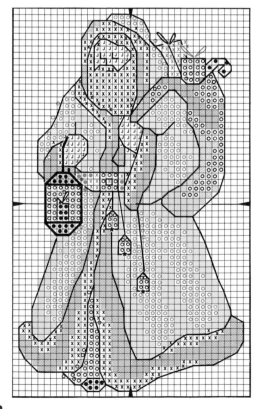

FABRIC: This ornament was stitched on Zweigart 18 count ivory Aida, color #264. A 5" x 6" piece is needed. For stitching, hold the fabric so the long sides run vertically.

CROSS-STITCH: Use two strands to stitch.

DETAILS: Use the number of strands indicated in parentheses.

Thin black lines — 3031 (1) Backstitch
Thin black loop — 3031 (1) Lazy Daisy
Black stars — 3031 (2) French Knots
Blue line — 502 (2) Straight Stitch
Blue loops — 502 (2) Lazy Daisies
Pink lines — 321 (2) Straight Stitch
Pink loops — 321 (2) Lazy Daisies
Thick black lines — 310 (2) Backstitch

FINISHING: Our model was assembled using method #1, Cardboard Cut-Out (see page 156). The edges were trimmed with ½" pregathered lace and pearls by the yard. The hanger and bow are ⅛" satin ribbon.

True Blue Santa

Finished Size: 2½" x 4"
33 x 53 Stitches

SYMBOL		COLOR	DMC	ANCHOR
J J	—	PALE PEACH	754	778
x x	—	PINK	760	8
● ●	—	RED	321	47
o o	—	CREAM	739	366
x x	—	GOLD	783	363
o o	—	GREEN	987	246
	—	BRIGHT BLUE	798	132
● ●	—	ROYAL BLUE	796	134
x x	—	TAN	738	367
o o	—	LT. BROWN	301	355
● ●	—	BROWN	3031	360
	—	WHITE	White	1

FABRIC: This ornament was stitched on Charles Craft 14 count antique white Aida. A 5" x 6" piece is needed. For stitching, hold the fabric so the long sides run vertically.

CROSS-STITCH: Use three strands to stitch.

DETAILS: Use the number of strands in parentheses.

Year — 321 (2) Backstitch: Use the numbers from Personalizing Chart #8 (see page 155).
Blue lines — 783 (3) Smyrna Cross-stitch
Black lines — 3031 (1) Backstitch

FINISHING: Our model was assembled using method #1, Cardboard Cut-Out (see page 156). The edges were trimmed with ¼" piping. Bows and a hanger made with ¼" satin ribbon were attached. Two bells were tacked to the bottom.

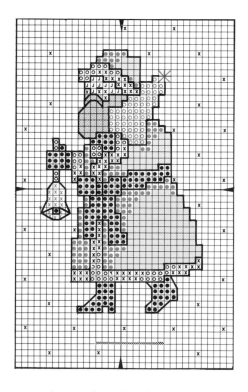

Kriss Kringle

Finished Size: 2" x 4"
28 x 59 Stitches

SYMBOL		COLOR	DMC	ANCHOR
	—	LT. PEACH	353	868
	—	PINK	894	26
	—	DK. RED	498	43
	—	MAROON	814	45
	—	DK. GREEN	986	246
	—	BROWN	300	352
		BLACK	310	403
	—	WHITE	White	1

NOTE: The color without a symbol is not used for Cross-stitch; it is used for details only.

FABRIC: This ornament was stitched on Wichelt Imports 14 count red Aida, color #954. A 4" x 6" piece is needed. For stitching, hold the fabric so the long sides run vertically.

CROSS-STITCH: Use three strands to stitch.

DETAILS: Use the number of strands indicated in parentheses.

    Black lines — 310 (1) Backstitch
    Pink heart — 498 (3) French Knot

The blue line at the edge of the design indicates the shape of the finished ornament.

FINISHING: Our model was assembled using method #1, Cardboard Cut-Out (see page 156). The edges were trimmed with ⅛" piping. The hanger and bow were added with ⅛" satin ribbon. A ½" jingle bell was tacked to the bottom.

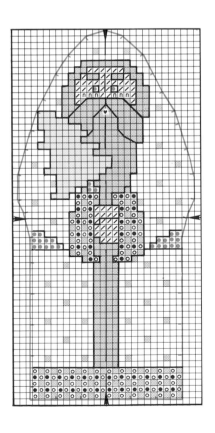

All-American Santa

Finished Size: 2¾" x 5¼"
40 x 64 Stitches

SYMBOL		COLOR	DMC	ANCHOR
o o	—	PALE PEACH	754	778
	—	RED	321	9046
x x	—	YELLOW	725	305
o o	—	BRIGHT BLUE	798	132
● o	—	ROYAL BLUE	796	134
o o	—	LT. BROWN	301	351
x x	—	BROWN	300	357
● ●	—	BLACK	310	403
	—	WHITE	White	1

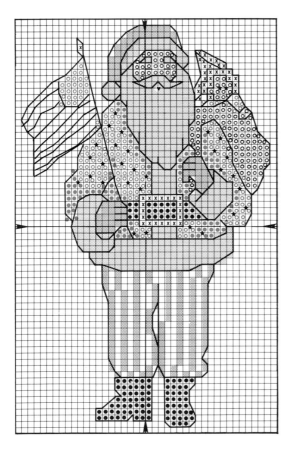

FABRIC: This ornament was stitched on Zweigart 18 count Floba, color #53. A 5" x 10" piece is needed. For stitching, hold the fabric so the long sides run vertically.

CROSS-STITCH: Use two strands to stitch.

DETAILS: Use the number of strands indicated in parentheses.

    Pink lines — 321 (2) Backstitch
    Pink heart — 321 (2) French Knot
    Pink stars — 725 (2) French Knots
    Black lines — 310 (1) Backstitch and Straight Stitch
    Black stars — 310 (1) French Knots

FINISHING: Our model was assembled with natural wood hardware using method #2, Bellpull Banner (see page 157). The Monk's Cording hanger was made with twelve strands of DMC #321.

Soaring Santa

Finished Size: 2¾" x 4½"
38 x 63 Stitches

SYMBOL			COLOR	DMC	ANCHOR
o	o	—	PALE PEACH	754	778
x	x	—	PINK	894	26
		—	RED	666	9046
●	●	—	DK. RED	498	44
o	o	—	YELLOW	725	305
		—	GREEN	702	227
●	●	—	DK. GREEN	699	923
		—	LT. BROWN	921	349
●	●	—	BLACK	310	403

FABRIC: This ornament was stitched on Zweigart 14 count white Aida. A 5" x 7" piece is needed. For stitching, hold the fabric so the long sides run vertically.

CROSS-STITCH: Use three strands to stitch.

DETAILS: Use the number of strands in parentheses.

Year — 310 (2) Backstitch: Use the numbers from Personalizing Chart #7 (see page 155).
Black lines — 310 (1) Backstitch
"MERRY CHRISTMAS" — 498 (2) Backstitch
Blue stars — 699 (6) French Knots

The blue line at the edge of the design indicates the shape of the finished ornament.

FINISHING: Our model was assembled using method #1, Cardboard Cut-Out (see page 156). The edges were trimmed with ⅛" piping. The hanger and bow were made of ⅛" satin ribbon. A ¼" pom-pom was glued to Santa's cap, and a ½" jingle bell was tacked to the bottom.

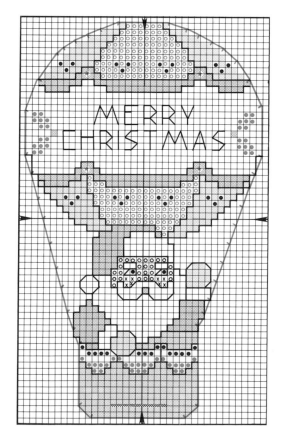

Père Noel

Finished Size: 3" Round
48 x 49 Stitches

SYMBOL	COLOR	DMC	ANCHOR
J J	CREAM	948	778
x x	PALE PEACH	754	868
x x	PINK	761	36
n n	PEACH	758	883
o o	RED ORANGE	350	335
	RED	817	47
● ●	MAROON	498	44
o o	LT. GREEN	989	257
	GREEN	987	258
● ●	DK. GREEN	500	246
o o	GRAY	647	233
	BROWN	3031	905
● ●	BLACK	310	403

FABRIC: This ornament was stitched on Zweigart 18 count ivory Aida, color #264. A 5" x 5" piece is needed.

CROSS-STITCH: Use two strands to stitch.

DETAILS: Use the number of strands indicated in parentheses.

    Pink lines — 498 (1) Backstitch
    Pink hearts — 498 (3) French Knots
    Black lines — 3031 (1) Backstitch

FINISHING: Our model was assembled using method #1, Cardboard Cut-Out (see page 156). The edges were trimmed with ⅛" satin cording. The hanger and bow were made with ⅜" grosgrain ribbon.

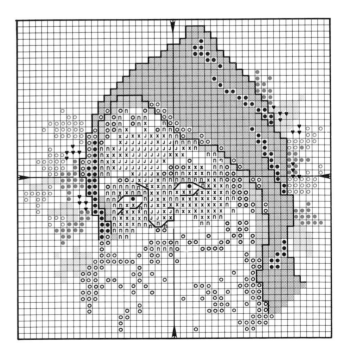

Legendary Santa

Finished Size: 3" x 4"
32 x 64 Stitches

SYMBOL		COLOR	DMC	ANCHOR
J J	—	PALE PEACH	754	778
o o	—	RED	321	47
	—	MAROON	816	20
n n	—	YELLOW	725	305
o o	—	GREEN	502	216
● ●	—	DK. GREEN	501	218
x x	—	BLUE	322	978
	—	ORANGE BROWN	921	349
o o	—	RED BROWN	920	351
x x	—	LT. GRAY BROWN	841	392
n n	—	DK. BROWN	3031	905
■ ■	—	BLACK	310	403

FABRIC: This ornament was stitched on Zweigart 18 count ivory Aida, color #264. A 5" x 6" piece is needed. For stitching, hold the fabric so the long sides run vertically.

CROSS-STITCH: Use two strands to stitch.

DETAILS: Use the number of strands indicated in parentheses.

Blue lines — 725 (2) Straight Stitch
Santa's eyes — 310 (2) Straight Stitch
All other black lines — 3031 (1) Backstitch
Black hearts — 3031 (1) French Knots

FINISHING: Our model was assembled using method #1, Cardboard Cut-Out (see page 156). The trim, hanger, and bow were made with ⅛" satin cording. Three small pinecones were glued to the top.

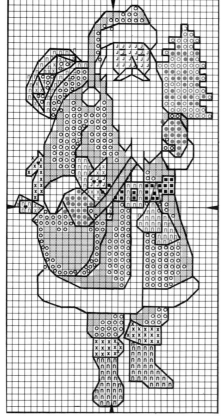

Roly-Poly Santa

Finished Size: 3" x 3¾"
41 x 46 Stitches

SYMBOL	COLOR	DMC	ANCHOR
ⁿⁿ —	PINK	760	26
—	RED	666	9046
╱╱ —	PALE PEACH	754	778
—	LT. PEACH	353	868
╱╱ —	YELLOW	726	289
—	GREEN	909	229
•• —	BLACK	310	403
—	WHITE	White	1

NOTE: The color without a symbol is not used for Cross-stitch; it is used for details only.

FABRIC: This ornament was stitched on Wichelt Imports 14 count red Aida, color #954. A 5" x 6" piece is needed. For stitching, hold the fabric so the long sides run vertically.

CROSS-STITCH: Use three strands to stitch.

DETAILS: Use the number of strands indicated in parentheses.

Pink lines — 666 (2) Backstitch and Straight Stitch
Black lines — 310 (1) Backstitch

The blue line at the edge of the design indicates the shape of the finished ornament.

FINISHING: Our model was assembled using method #1, Cardboard Cut-Out (see page 156). The edges were trimmed with ¼" piping. The hanger and bow were made with ⅛" satin ribbon. A ½" pom-pom was glued to the top, and a ½" jingle bell was tacked to the bottom.

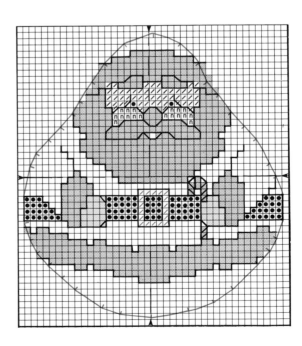

Turn-of-the Century Elegance

Gas lights, horses and carriages, tufted velvet furniture, candlelit Christmas trees ... beribboned and bejeweled ladies on the arms of elegantly turned out men. The turn of the century was a grand, opulent era that has provided us with a beautiful theme for holiday decorating.

Rosebud Heart

Finished Size: 3" x 2¾"
46 x 37 Stitches

SYMBOL	COLOR	DMC	ANCHOR
—	LT. PINK	776	24
—	PINK	3708	31
—	DK. PINK	3706	33
—	CORAL	3705	35
—	RED	321	9046
	GOLD	977	363
—	LT. GREEN	563	208
—	DK. GREEN	561	212
	LAVENDER	341	117
	BALGER® JAPAN GOLD #5		
	GOLD BEADS (quantity, 10)		

NOTE: The colors without symbols are not used for Cross-stitch; they are used for details only.

FABRIC: This ornament was stitched on Zweigart 18 count daffodil color damask Aida, color #202. A 5" x 5" piece is needed.

CROSS-STITCH: Use two strands to stitch.

DETAILS: Use the number of strands indicated in parentheses.

  Pink lines — 3705 (1) Backstitch
  Pink stars — 977 (3) French Knots
  Blue lines — 561 (1) Backstitch
  Blue stars — 341 (3) French Knots
  Thin black lines — 321 (1) Backstitch
  Thick black lines — Japan Gold (1)
    Straight Stitch
  Black stars — gold beads attached with
    977 (1)

FINISHING: Our model was assembled using method #1, Cardboard Cut-Out (see page 156). The edges were trimmed with ⅛" satin cording and 1" wide pregathered lace. The hanger and bow were made of ⅛" satin ribbon. A ½" ribbon rosette and a 1" tassel were added.

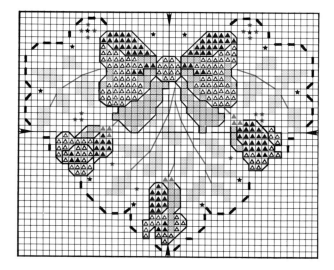

Rosebud Fan

Finished Size: 4" x 2"
64 x 31 Stitches

FABRIC: This ornament was stitched on Zweigart 18 count daffodil color damask Aida, color #202. A 6" x 4" piece is needed. For stitching, hold the fabric so the long sides run horizontally.

CROSS-STITCH: Use two strands to stitch.

DETAILS: Use the number of strands indicated in parentheses.

Pink lines — 321 (1) Backstitch
Blue lines — 561 (1) Backstitch
Blue stars — 341 (3) French Knots
Black lines — Japan Gold (1)
  Straight Stitch
Black stars — gold beads attached
  with 977 (1)

FINISHING: Our model was assembled using method #1, Cardboard Cut-Out (see page 156). The edges were trimmed with ⅛" satin cording and 1" wide pregathered lace. The hanger and bow were made of ⅛" satin ribbon. A ½" ribbon rosette and a 1" tassel were added.

SYMBOL	COLOR	DMC	ANCHOR
+	— Lt. Pink	776	24
△	— Pink	3708	31
▲	— Dk. Pink	3706	33
△	— Coral	3705	35
▲	— Red	321	9046
	Gold	977	363
▒	— Lt. Green	563	208
▲	— Dk. Green	561	212
	Lavender	341	117
	Balger® Japan Gold #5		
	Gold Beads (quantity, 13)		

NOTE: The colors without symbols are not used for Cross-stitch; they are used for details only.

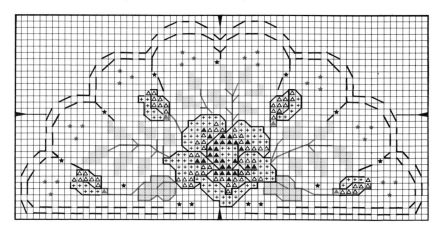

Rosebud Circle

Finished Size: 3½" Round
56 x 56 Stitches

SYMBOL		COLOR	DMC	ANCHOR
	—	PALE PINK	819	271
	—	LT. PINK	776	24
	—	PINK	3708	31
	—	DK. PINK	3706	33
	—	CORAL	3705	35
	—	RED	321	9046
		GOLD	977	363
	—	LT. GREEN	563	208
	—	DK. GREEN	561	212
		LAVENDER	341	117
		BALGER® JAPAN GOLD #5		
		GOLD BEADS (quantity, 16)		

NOTE: *The colors without symbols are not used for Cross-stitch; they are used for details only.*

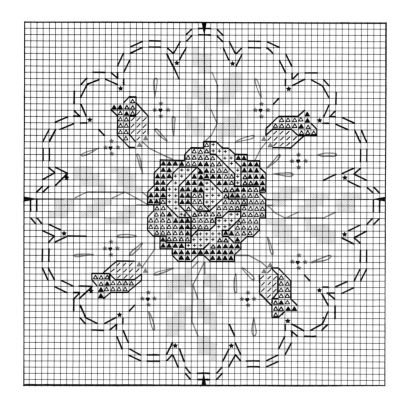

FABRIC: This ornament was stitched on Zweigart 18 count daffodil color damask Aida, color #202. A 6" x 6" piece is needed.

CROSS-STITCH: Use two strands to stitch.

DETAILS: Use the number of strands indicated in parentheses.

Pink lines — 321 (1) Backstitch
Black hearts — 977 (3) French Knots
Blue loops — 561 (1) Lazy Daisies
Blue lines — 561 (1) Backstitch
Blue stars — 341 (3) French Knots
Black lines — Japan Gold (1)
   Straight Stitch
Black stars — gold beads attached
   with 977 (1)

FINISHING: Our model was assembled using method #1, Cardboard Cut-Out (see page 156). The edges were trimmed with ⅛" satin cording and 1" pregathered lace. The hanger and bow were made of ⅛" satin ribbon. A ½" ribbon rosette and a 1" tassel were added.

Flame-stitch Rosebuds

Finished Size: 2½" x 3¼"
41 x 59 Stitches

SYMBOL		COLOR	DMC	ANCHOR
+ +	—	PALE PINK	819	271
△△	—	LT. PINK	776	24
	—	PINK	3708	31
+ +	—	DK. PINK	3706	33
△△	—	CORAL	3705	35
	—	RED	321	9046
		GOLD	977	363
△△	—	LT. GREEN	563	208
△△	—	DK. GREEN	561	212
		LAVENDER	341	117
		BALGER® JAPAN GOLD #5		
		GOLD BEADS (quantity, 12)		

NOTE: The colors without symbols are not used for Cross-stitch; they are used for details only.

FABRIC: This ornament was stitched on Zweigart 18 count daffodil color damask Aida, color #202. A 5" x 6" piece is needed. For stitching, hold the fabric so the long sides run vertically.

CROSS-STITCH: Use two strands to stitch.

DETAILS: Use the number of strands indicated in parentheses.

Black lines — 321 (1) Backstitch
Blue loops — 561 (1) Lazy Daisies
Blue lines — 561 (1) Backstitch
Blue stars — 341 (3) French Knots
Pink loops — Japan Gold (1) Lazy Daisies
Black stars — gold beads attached with 977 (1)

FINISHING: Our model was assembled using method #1, Cardboard Cut-Out (see page 156). The edges were trimmed with ⅛" satin cording. The hanger and bow were made of ⅛" satin ribbon. A ½" ribbon rosette and a 1" tassel were added.

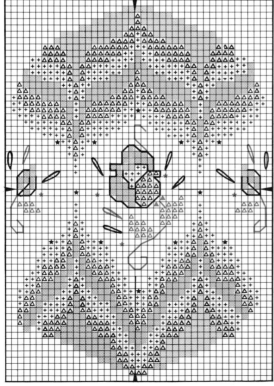

Crazy Quilt Fan

Finished Size: 4" x 2"
54 x 27 Stitches

SYMBOL		COLOR	DMC	ANCHOR
△△	—	Lt. Fuchsia	604	60
	—	Fuchsia	603	62
▲▲	—	Dk. Fuchsia	601	63
▲▲	—	Dk. Yellow	725	306
	—	Lt. Teal	959	185
▲▲	—	Teal	958	187
	—	Dk. Teal	943	188
△△	—	Cream	746	926

NOTE: The color without a symbol is not used for Cross-stitch; it is used for details only.

FABRIC: This ornament was stitched on Zweigart 14 count black Aida, color #95. A 6" x 4" piece is needed. For stitching, hold the fabric so the long sides run horizontally.

CROSS-STITCH: Use three strands to stitch.

DETAILS: Use the number of strands indicated in parentheses.

Blue lines — 943 (2) Straight Stitch
Blue loops — 943 (2) Lazy Daisies
Thin black lines — 746 (1) Backstitch
Thick black lines — 746 (2) Backstitch

FINISHING: Our model was assembled using method #1, Cardboard Cut-Out (see page 156). The edges were trimmed with ⅛" satin cording and ½" flat lace. The hanger and bow were made of ⅛" satin ribbon. A small pearl was glued to the center of the bow.

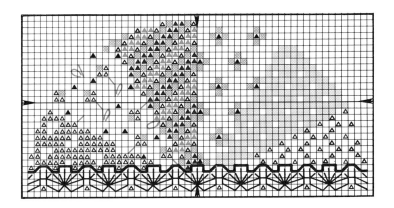

Crazy Quilt Stocking

Finished Size: 3" x 4"
42 x 55 Stitches

SYMBOL	COLOR	DMC	ANCHOR
—	Lt. Fuchsia	604	60
x x	Fuchsia	603	62
△△	Dk. Fuchsia	601	63
	Dk. Yellow	725	306
—	Lt. Teal	959	185
x x	Teal	958	187
	Dk. Teal	943	188
	Black	310	403
—	Cream	746	926

NOTE: The colors without symbols are not used for Cross-stitch; they are used for details only.

FABRIC: This ornament was stitched on Zweigart 14 count black Aida, color #95. A 5" x 6" piece is needed. For stitching, hold the fabric so the long sides run vertically.

CROSS-STITCH: Use three strands to stitch.

DETAILS: Use the number of strands indicated in parentheses.

Blue lines — 725 (2) Backstitch
Blue open stars — 725 (2) French Knots
Thin black lines — 943 (1) Straight Stitch
Black loops — 943 (1) Lazy Daisies
Thick black lines — 310 (1) Straight Stitch
Black solid stars — 310 (3) French Knots
Thin pink lines — 746 (1) Straight Stitch
Thick pink lines — 746 (2) Backstitch

FINISHING: Our model was assembled using method #1, Cardboard Cut-Out (see page 156). The top edge was trimmed with ½" flat lace. Satin cording ⅛" wide was used to trim the edges and make the hanger. The bow was made of ⅛" satin ribbon. A small pearl was glued to the center of the bow.

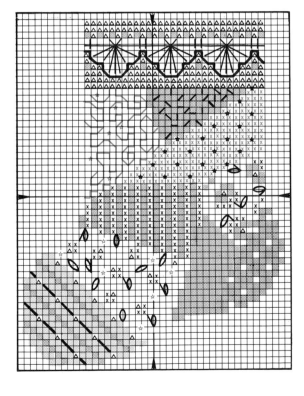

Crazy Quilt Heart

Finished Size: 4" x 3¼"
55 x 44 Stitches

SYMBOL		COLOR	DMC	ANCHOR
x x	—	LT. FUCHSIA	604	60
△ △	—	FUCHSIA	603	62
▲ ▲	—	DK. FUCHSIA	601	63
△ △	—	DK. YELLOW	725	306
	—	TEAL	958	187
▲ ▲	—	DK. TEAL	943	188
	—	CREAM	746	926
		BALGER® JAPAN GOLD #5		

NOTE: The color without a symbol is not used for Cross-stitch; it is used for details only.

FABRIC: This ornament was stitched on Zweigart 14 count black Aida, color #95. A 6" x 6" piece is needed.

CROSS-STITCH: Use three strands to stitch.

DETAILS: Use the number of strands indicated in parentheses.

Thin blue lines — 958 (1) Backstitch
Thin blue loops — 943 (2) Lazy Daisies
Thick blue lines — 943 (2) Backstitch
Thin pink lines — 601 (2) Backstitch
Date — Japan Gold (2) Backstitch: Use
   Personalizing Chart #6 (see page 154).
Thick pink lines — Japan Gold (2) Backstitch
Thin black lines — 746 (1) Straight Stitch
Thick black lines — 746 (2) Backstitch

FINISHING: Our model was assembled using method #1, Cardboard Cut-Out (see page 156). The edges were trimmed with ⅛" satin cording and ½" flat lace. The hanger and bow were made of ⅛" satin ribbon. A small pearl was glued to the center of the bow.

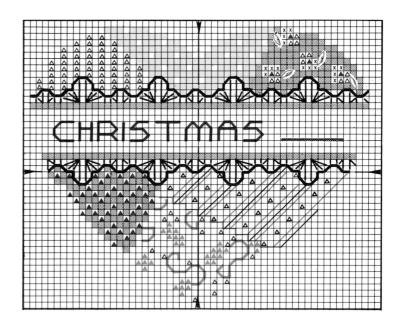

Gilded Noel

Finished Size: 3" Round
42 x 42 Stitches

SYMBOL		COLOR	DMC	ANCHOR
	—	CREAM	712	387
	—	BALGER® JAPAN GOLD #5		

FABRIC: This ornament was stitched on Charles Craft 14 count emerald-green Aida. A 5" x 5" piece is needed.

CROSS-STITCH: Use three strands of #712. Use two strands of Japan Gold.

DETAILS: Use the number of strands indicated in parentheses.

    Blue lines — 712 (2) Backstitch
    Thin black lines — 712 (1) Straight Stitch
    Pink lines — Japan Gold (1) Backstitch
    Pink loops — Japan Gold (1) Lazy Daisies
    Thick black lines — Japan Gold (2) Backstitch

FINISHING: Our model was assembled using method #1, Cardboard Cut-Out (see page 156). The hanger was made of Monk's Cording using two strands of Japan Gold. The edges were trimmed with ⅛" satin cording and ¾" gold metallic lace. A bow made of ⅜" satin ribbon was added.

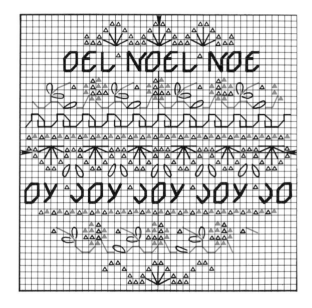

Sparkling Snowflake

Finished Size: 3" Round
41 x 41 Stitches

SYMBOL	COLOR	DMC	ANCHOR
—	CREAM	712	387
—	BALGER® JAPAN GOLD #5		

FABRIC: This ornament was stitched on Charles Craft 14 count emerald-green Aida. A 5" x 5" piece is needed.

CROSS-STITCH: Use three strands of #712. Use two strands of Japan Gold.

DETAILS: Use the number of strands indicated in parentheses.

    Blue lines — Japan Gold (1) Backstitch
    Pink lines — Japan Gold (2) Backstitch
    Black lines — 712 (3) Backstitch

FINISHING: Our model was assembled using method #1, Cardboard Cut-Out (see page 156). The hanger was made of Monk's Cording using two strands of Japan Gold. The edges were trimmed with ⅛" satin cording and ¾" gold metallic lace. A bow made of ⅜" satin ribbon was added.

Glittering Snowflake

Finished Size: 3" Round
41 x 41 Stitches

SYMBOL	COLOR	DMC	ANCHOR
△△ —	CREAM	712	387
▲▲ —	BALGER® JAPAN GOLD #5		

FABRIC: This ornament was stitched on Charles Craft 14 count emerald-green Aida. A 5" x 5" piece is needed.

CROSS-STITCH: Use three strands of #712. Use two strands of Japan Gold.

DETAILS: Use the number of strands indicated in parentheses.

Blue lines — Japan Gold (1) Backstitch
Pink lines — Japan Gold (2) Backstitch
Black lines — 712 (3) Backstitch

FINISHING: Our model was assembled using method #1, Cardboard Cut-Out (see page 156). The hanger was made of Monk's Cording using two strands of Japan Gold. The edges were trimmed with ⅛" satin cording and ¾" gold metallic lace. A bow made of ⅜" satin ribbon was added.

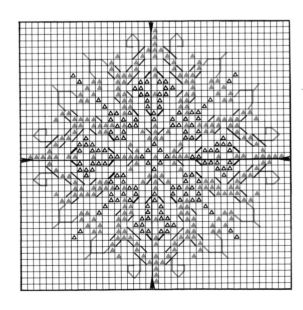

Teddy Bears for All Ages

Brightly colored bears, antique bears, silly bears, cuddly bears ... teddy bears are a favorite toy whatever your age. Whether you are rekindling memories of past holidays or making new ones, there's always room in your heart for another lovable teddy bear!

Waiting for Santa

Finished Size: 2½" x 4¼"
31 x 52 Stitches

SYMBOL		COLOR	DMC	ANCHOR
⊞	—	DK. RED	321	9046
●●	—	WINE	498	44
		YELLOW	743	305
⊙⊙	—	LIME GREEN	703	238
⊡	—	BRIGHT GREEN	700	229
	—	TURQUOISE	807	168
○○	—	PALE PEACH	951	366
▦	—	RUST	922	349
●●	—	DK. RED BROWN	920	351
✗✗	—	DK. BROWN	3371	382

NOTE: The color without a symbol was not used for Cross-stitch; it was used for details only.

FABRIC: This ornament was stitched on Wichelt Imports 14 count dk. blue Aida, color #567. A 5" x 6" piece is needed. For stitching, hold the fabric so the long sides run vertically.

CROSS-STITCH: Use three strands to stitch.

DETAILS: Use the number of strands indicated in parentheses.

Pink stars — 321 (3) French Knots
Blue lines — 743 (3) Backstitch
Black lines — 3371 (1) Backstitch

FINISHING: Our model was assembled using method #1, Cardboard Cut-Out (see page 156). The edges were trimmed with two rows of ⅛" piping. The bow and hanger were made of ⅛" satin ribbon.

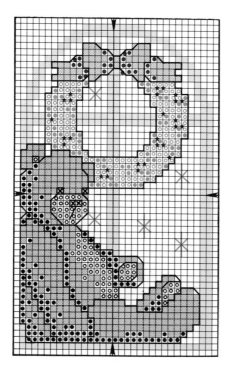

The Woodsman

Finished Size: 2½" x 4¼"
35 x 50 Stitches

SYMBOL	COLOR	DMC	ANCHOR
●● —	RED	666	46
—	WINE	817	47
—	ORANGE	970	316
○○ —	DK. YELLOW	744	305
○○ —	GOLD	977	363
✕✕ —	GREEN	702	226
—	DK. GREEN	699	923
●● —	TURQUOISE	807	168
●● —	PURPLE	552	101
○○ —	RUST	921	351
—	BLACK	310	403

NOTE: The colors without symbols are not used for Cross-stitch; they are used for details only.

FABRIC: This ornament was stitched on Zweigart 14 count ivory Aida, color #264. A 5" x 9" piece is needed. For stitching, hold the fabric so the long sides run vertically.

CROSS-STITCH: Use three strands to stitch.

DETAILS: Use the number of strands indicated in parentheses.

Date — 666 (2) Backstitch: Use the numbers from Personalizing Chart #6 (see page 154).
Pink lines — 817 (2) Backstitch
Black lines — 310 (1) Backstitch
Black stars — 310 (3) French Knots
Blue lines — 552 (2) Straight Stitch

FINISHING: Our model was assembled with natural wood hardware using method #2, Bellpull Banner (see page 157). The cording for the hanger was made with twelve strands of DMC #817.

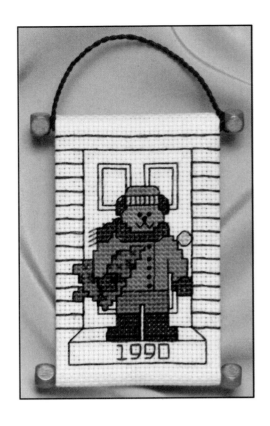

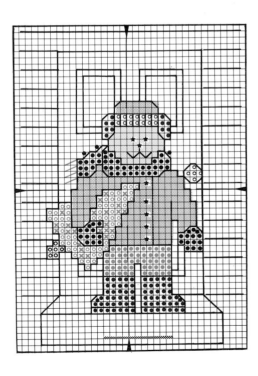

Jean-Claude Bearly

Finished Size: 4¼" x 4¼"
45 x 40 Stitches

SYMBOL		COLOR	DMC	ANCHOR
● ●	—	DEEP PINK	891	28
	—	RED	666	46
○ ○	—	YELLOW	743	305
○ ○	—	MINT GREEN	954	203
✕ ✕	—	GREEN	911	230
● ●	—	LT. BLUE	809	129
	—	PURPLE	552	101
○ ○	—	LT. RUST	922	349
● ●	—	BROWN	3031	360

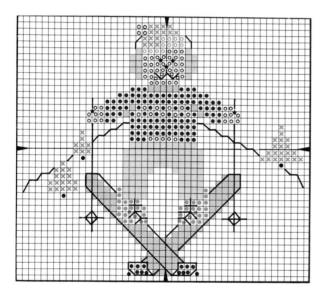

FABRIC: This ornament was stitched on Zweigart 14 count white Aida, color #1. A 6" x 6" piece is needed.

CROSS-STITCH: Use three strands to stitch.

DETAILS: Use the number of strands indicated in parentheses.

Pink lines — 666 (3) Backstitch
Black lines — 3031 (1) Backstitch
Black stars — 3031 (3) French Knots
Add a ¼ " yellow pom-pom to the bear's hat.

FINISHING: Our model was assembled using method #1, Cardboard Cut-Out (see page 156). It was trimmed with two rows of ⅛" piping, a ¾" jingle bell, and a hanger and bow of ⅛" satin ribbon.

Checkerboard Bear

Finished Size: 2" x 5"
25 x 47 Stitches

SYMBOL	COLOR	DMC	ANCHOR
◨ —	Dk. Red	321	9046
	Spruce	501	878
▦ —	Tan	437	362
	Brown	3031	360

NOTE: The colors without symbols are not used for Cross-stitch; they are used for details only.

FABRIC: This ornament was stitched on Zweigart 25 count raw Dublin linen, color #53. A 4" x 7" piece is needed. For stitching, hold the fabric so the long sides run vertically.

CROSS-STITCH: Use three strands to stitch. Work each Cross-stitch over two fabric threads.

DETAILS: Use the number of strands indicated in parentheses.
Blue lines — 501 (2) Backstitch
Black lines — 3031 (1) Backstitch and Straight Stitch
Black stars — 3031 (3) French Knots

FINISHING: Our model was assembled using method #3, Fringed Banner (see page 158). The hanger and bow were made of 1/16" ribbon.

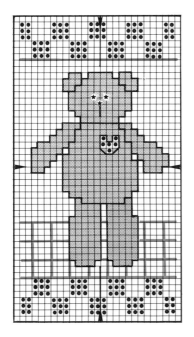

Wind-Up Bear

Finished Size: 2½" x 4¾"
33 x 52 Stitches

SYMBOL	COLOR	DMC	ANCHOR
—	PINK	899	75
—	RED	666	46
—	DK. YELLOW	725	306
—	GREEN	700	229
—	TURQUOISE	807	168
—	PURPLE	553	99
—	GOLDEN BROWN	435	365
—	BLACK	310	403

FABRIC: This ornament was stitched on Zweigart 14 count white Aida, color #1. A 5" x 9" piece is needed. For stitching, hold the fabric so the long sides run vertically.

CROSS-STITCH: Use three strands to stitch.

DETAILS: Use the number of strands indicated in parentheses.

Name — 666 (3) Backstitch: Use the letters from Personalizing Chart #9 (see page 155).
Black lines in borders — 310 (1) Straight Stitch
Remaining black lines — 310 (1) Backstitch
Black stars — 310 (3) French Knots

FINISHING: Our model was assembled with natural wood hardware using method #2, Bellpull Banner (see page 157). The hanger and bow were made of ⅛" satin ribbon.

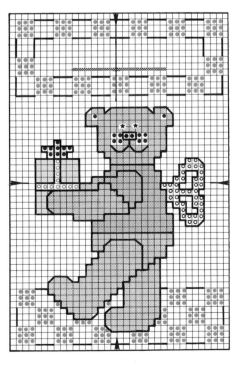

Beary Best Friends

Finished Size: 3¾" x 3¼"
33 x 31 Stitches

SYMBOL	COLOR	DMC	ANCHOR
—	LT. RED	350	13
—	DK. RED	817	47
—	PALE RUST	402	347
—	LT. RUST	922	349
—	OLIVE GREEN	905	258
—	LT. TAUPE	842	376
—	TAUPE	840	379
	DK. BROWN	3371	382

NOTE: The color without a symbol is not used for Cross-stitch; it is used for details only.

FABRIC: This ornament was stitched on Zweigart 25 count raw Dublin linen, color #53. A 6" x 6" piece is needed.

CROSS-STITCH: Use three strands to stitch. Work each Cross-stitch over two fabric threads.

DETAILS: Use the number of strands indicated in parentheses.

Date — 817 (2) Backstitch: Use the numbers from Personalizing Chart #10 (see page 155).
Black lines — 3371 (1) Backstitch and Straight Stitch
Black stars — 3371 (3) French Knots

FINISHING: Our model was assembled using method #1, Cardboard Cut-Out (see page 156). The edges were trimmed with ¼" satin cording and a 3" tassel. The hanger and bow were made of ⅛" satin ribbon.

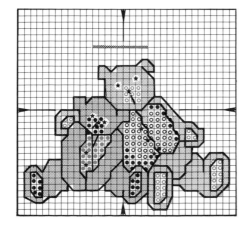

Stocking Bear

Finished Size: 3" x 4"
39 x 52 Stitches

SYMBOL		COLOR	DMC	ANCHOR
○○ ○○	—	DEEP PINK	891	28
●● ●●	—	RED	666	46
○○ ○○	—	LEMON	726	295
	—	LIME GREEN	703	238
●○ ○●	—	BLUE	312	979
	—	LT. RED BROWN	976	349
	—	RED BROWN	975	351
		BLACK	310	403
○○	—	WHITE	White	1

NOTE: The color without a symbol is not used for Cross-stitch; it is used for details only.

FABRIC: This ornament was stitched on Zweigart 14 count oatmeal Rustico, color #54. A 5" x 7" piece is needed. For stitching, hold the fabric so the long sides run vertically.

CROSS-STITCH: Use three strands to stitch.

DETAILS: Use the number of strands indicated in parentheses.

Black lines — 310 (1) Backstitch and Straight Stitch
Black stars — 310 (3) French Knots
Attach a ¼" jingle bell to the tip of the bear's hat with 666 (2).

FINISHING: Our model was assembled using method #1, Cardboard Cut-Out (see page 156). The edges were trimmed with ⅛" piping and a ¾" jingle bell. The hanger and bow were made of ⅛" satin ribbon.

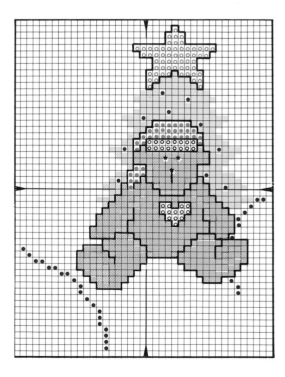

Joyful Tidings Bear

Finished Size: 4" x 3"
43 x 31 Stitches

SYMBOL	COLOR	DMC	ANCHOR
	PINK	3326	31
	RED	666	46
	LIME GREEN	703	258
	BRIGHT GREEN	909	923
	BLUE	312	979
	PALE RUST	402	347
	LT. RUST	922	349
	BROWN	3031	360
	WHITE	White	1

NOTE: The colors without symbols are not used for Cross-stitch; they are used for details only.

FABRIC: This ornament was stitched on Zweigart 14 count lt. blue Aida, color #503. A 7" x 6" piece is needed. For stitching, hold the fabric so the long sides run horizontally.

CROSS-STITCH: Use three strands to stitch.

DETAILS: Use the number of strands indicated in parentheses.

Blue lines — 312 (2) Backstitch
Black lines — 3031 (1) Backstitch
Black stars — 3031 (3) French Knots

FINISHING: Our model was assembled using method #1, Cardboard Cut-Out (see page 156). The edges were trimmed with ¼" satin cording and a ½" eyelet lace ruffle. The bow and hanger were made of ¼" satin ribbon.

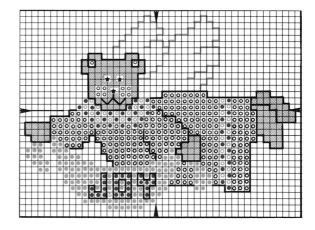

Santa Bear

Finished Size: 3¾" x 3¼"
32 x 31 Stitches

SYMBOL	COLOR	DMC	ANCHOR
—	BRICK RED	347	19
—	GRAY GREEN	503	875
—	SPRUCE	501	878
—	ECRU	Ecru	926
—	TAN	738	372
—	RED BROWN	435	365
	BROWN	3031	360
—	BLACK	310	403
—	WHITE	White	1

NOTE: The color without a symbol is not used for Cross-stitch; it is used for details only.

FABRIC: This ornament was stitched on Zweigart 14 count khaki Aida, color #740. A 6" x 6" piece is needed.

CROSS-STITCH: Use three strands to stitch.

DETAILS: Use the number of strands indicated in parentheses.

Pink lines — 310 (1) Backstitch
Thick black lines — 310 (2) Backstitch
Black hearts — 310 (2) French Knots
Black stars — 310 (3) French Knots
Thin black lines — 3031 (1) Backstitch

FINISHING: Our model was assembled using method #1, Cardboard Cut-Out (see page 156). The edges were trimmed with ⅛" piping and a 1" fabric ruffle. The hanger and bow were made of ⅛" satin ribbon.

Baby New Year

Finished Size: 2" x 4"
25 x 43 Stitches

SYMBOL		COLOR	DMC	ANCHOR
		RED	666	46
o o	—	LIME GREEN	704	256
+ +	—	TAN	738	372
▨	—	LT. RED BROWN	976	369
● ●	—	RED BROWN	975	371
		BLACK	310	403

NOTE: The colors without symbols are not used for Cross-stitch; they are used for details only.

FABRIC: This ornament was stitched on Zweigart 14 count white Aida, color #1. A 5" x 7" piece is needed. For stitching, hold the fabric so the long sides run vertically.

CROSS-STITCH: Use three strands to stitch.

DETAILS: Use the number of strands indicated in parentheses.

Date — 310 (2) Backstitch: Use the numbers from Personalizing Chart #4 (see page 154).
Letters — 666 (2) Backstitch
Black lines — 310 (1) Backstitch and Straight Stitch
Black stars — 310 (3) French Knots

FINISHING: Our model was assembled using method #1, Cardboard Cut-Out (see page 156). The edges were trimmed with ⅛" piping. The hanger and bow were made of ⅛" gold metallic ribbon. A gold star, wire, and safety pin were used as accents.

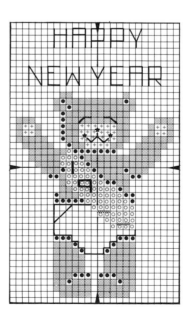

The True Meaning of Christmas

The Star of Bethlehem lit the night sky with joy and wonderment. The Magi brought gifts to the newborn Savior. The Herald Angel trumpeted the great and glorious news of the newborn Christ Child. As beautiful and joyful as it was then ... the True Meaning of Christmas.

Christmas Chapel

Finished Size: 2½" x 4¼"
39 x 65 Stitches

SYMBOL		COLOR	DMC	ANCHOR
x x	—	RED	349	46
+ +	—	YELLOW	725	306
x x	—	GREEN	987	245
	—	DK. GREEN	986	246
■ ■	—	GOLD	977	363
	—	RUST	921	370
		BLACK	310	403
▨	—	WHITE	White	1
		BALGER® JAPAN GOLD #5		

NOTE: The colors without symbols are not used for Cross-stitch; they are used for details only.

FABRIC: This ornament was stitched on Zweigart 18 count colonial blue Davosa, color #522. A 5" x 6" piece is needed. For stitching, hold the fabric so the long sides run vertically.

CROSS-STITCH: Use two strands to stitch.

DETAILS: Use the number of strands indicated in parentheses.

  Thin black lines — 310 (1) Backstitch
  Thick black lines — Japan Gold (1) Backstitch
  Blue lines — 986 (1) Backstitch
  Black hearts — 349 (2) French Knots
  Pink lines — 349 (2) Backstitch

FINISHING: Our model was assembled using method #1, Cardboard Cut-Out (see page 156). The edges were trimmed with ⅛" satin cording and Monk's Cording made with four strands of Japan Gold. The hanger was made with ⅛" satin ribbon.

Candlelit Scripture

Finished Size: 3½" x 2¾"
54 x 39 Stitches

SYMBOL		COLOR	DMC	ANCHOR
	—	RED	349	46
+ +	—	YELLOW	744	293
x x	—	PALE GREEN	966	206
	—	DK. GREEN	986	246
x x	—	GOLD	977	363
■ ■	—	BLACK	310	403
	—	WHITE	White	1
o o	—	BALGER® JAPAN GOLD #5		

FABRIC: This ornament was stitched on Zweigart 18 count colonial blue Davosa, color #522. A 6" x 5" piece is needed. For stitching, hold the fabric so the long sides run horizontally.

CROSS-STITCH: Use two strands to stitch.

DETAILS: Use the number of strands indicated in parentheses.

Pink lines — Japan Gold (2) Backstitch
Pink hearts — Japan Gold (2) French Knots
Blue lines — 986 (2) Backstitch
Black lines — 310 (1) Backstitch
Black hearts — 349 (3) French Knots

FINISHING: Our model was assembled using method #1, Cardboard Cut-Out (see page 156). The edges were trimmed with ⅛" satin cording and Monk's Cording made with four strands of Japan Gold. The hanger was made with ⅛" satin ribbon.

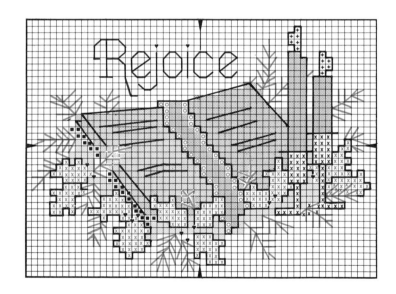

The Herald Angel

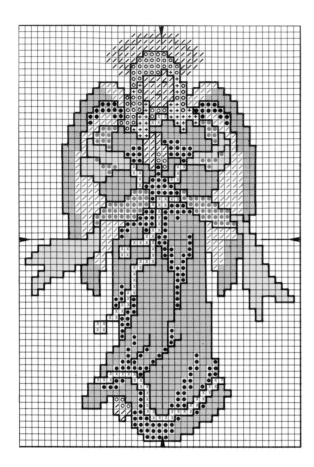

Finished Size: 3" x 4"
43 x 65 Stitches

SYMBOL	COLOR	DMC	ANCHOR
⁄⁄ —	PALE PEACH	754	6
o o —	PEACH	353	8
	PALE YELLOW	745	292
⁄⁄ —	PALE BLUE	775	128
● ● —	BLUE	809	130
▦ —	LT. ORCHID	3609	85
● ● —	ORCHID	3607	87
	LT. PURPLE	554	109
	PURPLE	553	111
o o —	LT. RUST	922	349
+ + —	RUST	301	884
	BROWN	801	360
x x —	BALGER® JAPAN GOLD #5		
▦ —	BALGER® PEARL #032		
	BALGER® STAR YELLOW #091		
	BALGER® STAR MAUVE #093		

BLENDED CROSS-STITCH — Two colors are threaded together in the needle to produce a lustrous effect.

⁄⁄ —	1 strand of 745; 1 strand of 091	
—	1 strand of 554; 1 strand of 093	
● ● —	1 strand of 553; 1 strand of 093	

NOTE: The colors without symbols are not used for Cross-stitch; they are used for Blended Cross-stitch or details only.

FABRIC: This ornament was stitched on Charles Craft 18 count antique white Aida. A 5" x 6" piece is needed. For stitching, hold the fabric so the long sides run vertically.

CROSS-STITCH: Use two strands to stitch.

DETAILS: Use the number of strands indicated in parentheses.

Black lines — 801 (1) Backstitch and Straight Stitch
Blue lines — Japan Gold (1) Backstitch

FINISHING: Our model was assembled using method #1, Cardboard Cut-Out (see page 156). The edges were trimmed with ¹⁄₁₆" gold metallic cord and Monk's Cording made with thirty-six strands of DMC #553. The hanger and bow were made of ¼" satin ribbon.

Madonna and Child

Finished Size: 3" x 4"
48 x 65 Stitches

SYMBOL		COLOR	DMC	ANCHOR
☑☑	—	PALE PEACH	754	6
+|+	—	PEACH	353	8
		PALE YELLOW	745	292
╱╱	—	PALE BLUE	775	128
	—	BLUE	809	130
○○	—	DK. BLUE	798	142
╱╱	—	LT. ORCHID	3609	85
○○	—	ORCHID	3607	87
	—	LT. PURPLE	554	109
●●	—	PURPLE	553	111
○○	—	LT. RUST	922	349
●●	—	RUST	301	884
		BROWN	801	360
		BALGER® JAPAN GOLD #5		
x|x	—	BALGER® STAR YELLOW #091		

BLENDED CROSS-STITCH — Two colors are threaded together in the needle to produce a lustrous effect.

	—	1 strand of 745; 1 strand of 091

NOTE: The colors without symbols are not used for Cross-stitch; they are used for Blended Cross-stitch or details only.

FABRIC: This ornament was stitched on Charles Craft 18 count antique white Aida. A 5" x 6" piece is needed. For stitching, hold the fabric so the long sides run vertically.

CROSS-STITCH: Use two strands to stitch.

DETAILS: Use the number of strands indicated in parentheses.

    Black lines — 801 (1) Backstitch
    Black stars — 801 (2) French Knots
    Blue lines — Japan Gold (1) Backstitch

FINISHING: Our model was assembled using method #1, Cardboard Cut-Out (see page 156). The edges were trimmed with ¹⁄₁₆" gold metallic cord and Monk's Cording made with thirty-six strands of DMC #553. The hanger and bow were made of ¼" satin ribbon.

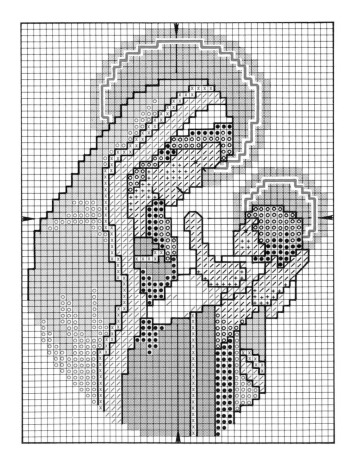

Manger Scene

Finished Size: 4" x 3"
56 x 46 Stitches

SYMBOL		COLOR	DMC	ANCHOR
⁄⁄	—	PALE PEACH	754	6
n n	—	PEACH	353	8
		PALE YELLOW	745	292
▒	—	GOLD	977	363
x x	—	DK. GOLD	976	365
	—	BLUE	800	129
● ●	—	DK. BLUE	799	145
⁄⁄	—	LT. ORCHID	3609	85
n n	—	ORCHID	3607	87
o o	—	LT. PURPLE	554	109
■ ■	—	PURPLE	553	111
+ +	—	CREAM	739	933
x x	—	LT. RUST	922	349
▒	—	RUST	301	884
		BROWN	801	360
		BALGER® JAPAN GOLD #5		
		BALGER® STAR YELLOW #091		

BLENDED CROSS-STITCH — Two colors are threaded together in the needle to produce a lustrous effect.

⁄⁄	—	1 strand of 745; 1 strand of 091

NOTE: The colors without symbols are not used for Cross-stitch; they are used for Blended Cross-stitch or details only.

FABRIC: This ornament was stitched on Charles Craft 18 count antique white Aida. A 6" x 5" piece is needed. For stitching, hold the fabric so the long sides run horizontally.

CROSS-STITCH: Use two strands to stitch.

DETAILS: Use the number of strands indicated in parentheses.

Thin black lines — 801 (1) Backstitch
Thick black lines — Japan Gold (1) Backstitch
Black stars — 801 (2) French Knots

FINISHING: Our model was assembled using method #1, Cardboard Cut-Out (see page 156). The edges were trimmed with ¹⁄₁₆" gold metallic cord and Monk's Cording made with thirty-six strands of DMC #553. The hanger and bow were made of ¼" satin ribbon.

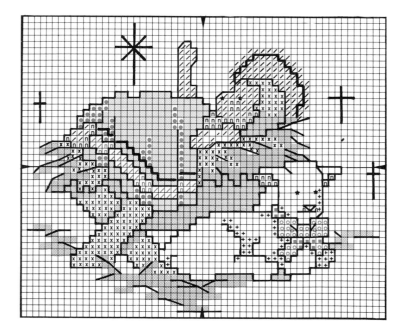

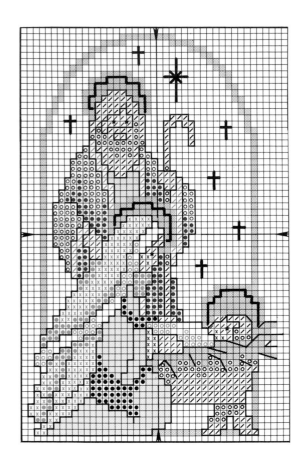

The Holy Family

Finished Size: 2½" x 4¼"
41 x 64 Stitches

SYMBOL	COLOR	DMC	ANCHOR
⊙⊙	RED	666	9046
●●	WINE	817	47
∕∕	PALE PEACH	754	6
✗✗	PEACH	353	8
	PALE YELLOW	745	292
▓	GOLD	977	363
∕∕	GREEN	3347	266
⊙⊙	PALE BLUE	775	128
✗✗	BLUE	809	130
●●	DK. BLUE	798	142
	LAVENDER	554	109
●●	PURPLE	553	111
∕∕	LT. RUST	922	349
⊙⊙	RUST	301	884
	BROWN	801	360
	BALGER® JAPAN GOLD #5		
	BALGER® STAR YELLOW #091		

BLENDED CROSS-STITCH — Two colors are threaded together in the needle to produce a lustrous effect.

▓	—	1 strand of 745; 1 strand of 091

NOTE: The colors without symbols are not used for Cross-stitch; they are used for Blended Cross-stitch or details only.

FABRIC: This ornament was stitched on Charles Craft 18 count antique white Aida. A 5" x 6" piece is needed. For stitching, hold the fabric so the long sides run vertically.

CROSS-STITCH: Use two strands to stitch.

DETAILS: Use the number of strands indicated in parentheses.

  Thin black lines — 801 (1) Backstitch
  Black stars — 801 (2) French Knots
  Thick black lines — Japan Gold (1) Backstitch

FINISHING: Our model was assembled using method #1, Cardboard Cut-Out (see page 156). The edges were trimmed with ¹⁄₁₆" gold metallic cord and Monk's Cording made with thirty-six strands of DMC #553. The hanger and bow were made of ¼" satin ribbon.

Gifts of the Magi

Finished Size: 3" x 4"
41 x 60 Stitches

SYMBOL	COLOR	DMC	ANCHOR
	RED	666	9046
	WINE	817	47
	PALE PEACH	754	6
	LT. GREEN	3347	266
	DK. GREEN	3345	268
	PALE BLUE	775	128
	BLUE	800	129
	DK. BLUE	798	142
	LT. ORCHID	3609	85
	ORCHID	3607	87
	LT. PURPLE	554	109
	PURPLE	553	111
	LT. RUST	922	349
	RUST	301	884
	BROWN	801	360
	BALGER® JAPAN GOLD #5		

NOTE: The color without a symbol is not used for Cross-stitch; it is used for details only.

FABRIC: This ornament was stitched on Charles Craft 18 count antique white Aida. A 5" x 6" piece is needed. For stitching, hold the fabric so the long sides run vertically.

CROSS-STITCH: Use two strands to stitch.

DETAILS: Use the number of strands indicated in parentheses.

Black lines — 801 (1) Backstitch and Straight Stitch
Blue stars — 801 (1) French Knots

FINISHING: Our model was assembled using method #1, Cardboard Cut-Out (see page 156). The edges were trimmed with 1/16" gold metallic cord and Monk's Cording made with thirty-six strands of DMC #553. The hanger and bow were made of 1/4" satin ribbon.

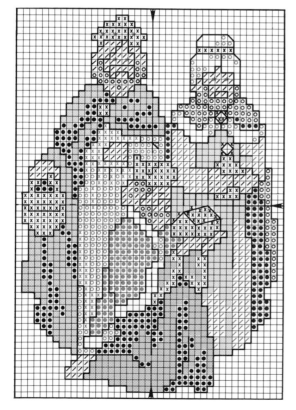

Stained Glass Joy

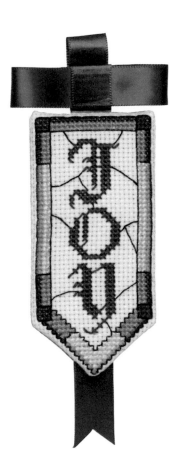

Finished Size: 2" x 4¼"
25 x 56 Stitches

SYMBOL	COLOR	DMC	ANCHOR
—	RED	349	46
—	GOLD	741	314
—	YELLOW	743	297
—	LT. GREEN	703	238
—	GREEN	700	228
—	BLUE	798	142
	BLACK	310	403

NOTE: The color without a symbol is not used for Cross-stitch; it is used for details only.

FABRIC: This ornament was stitched on Zweigart 14 count white Aida. A 4" x 6" piece is needed. For stitching, hold the fabric so the long sides run vertically.

CROSS-STITCH: Use three strands to stitch.

DETAILS: Use the number of strands indicated in parentheses.

Thick black lines — 798 (3) Backstitch
Thin black lines — 310 (1) Backstitch

FINISHING: Our model was assembled using method #1, Cardboard Cut-Out (see page 156). The hanger and bow were made of ⅝" satin ribbon.

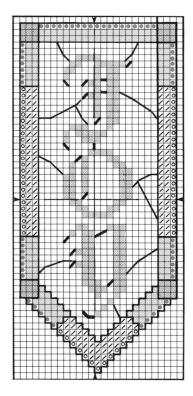

Stained Glass Dove

Finished Size: 3" x 3"
37 x 37 Stitches

SYMBOL	COLOR	DMC	ANCHOR
—	RED	349	46
—	GOLD	741	314
—	GREEN	703	238
—	BLUE	809	130
—	BLACK	310	403

FABRIC: This ornament was stitched on Zweigart 14 count white Aida. A 5" x 5" piece is needed.

CROSS-STITCH: Use three strands to stitch.

DETAILS: Use the number of strands indicated in parentheses.

Black star — 310 (3) French Knot
Black lines — 310 (1) Backstitch

FINISHING: Our model was assembled using method #1, Cardboard Cut-Out (see page 156). The hanger and bow were made of ⅝" satin ribbon.

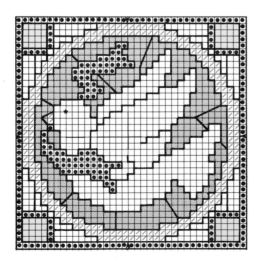

Stained Glass Candles

Finished Size: 3" x 3"
37 x 37 Stitches

SYMBOL		COLOR	DMC	ANCHOR
	—	RED	349	46
●●	—	WINE	816	20
○○	—	GOLD	741	314
╱╱	—	YELLOW	743	297
○○	—	LT. GREEN	703	238
	—	GREEN	702	239
●●	—	DK. GREEN	699	923
	—	LT. PURPLE	554	109
●●	—	PURPLE	553	111
		BLACK	310	403

NOTE: The color without a symbol is not used for Cross-stitch; it is used for details only.

FABRIC: This ornament was stitched on Zweigart 14 count white Aida. A 5" x 5" piece is needed.

CROSS-STITCH: Use three strands to stitch.

DETAILS: Use the number of strands indicated in parentheses.

Black lines — 310 (1) Backstitch

FINISHING: Our model was assembled using method #1, Cardboard Cut-Out (see page 156). The hanger and bow were made of ⅝" satin ribbon.

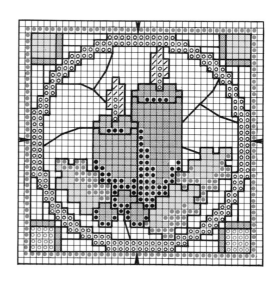

The True Meaning of Christmas   **83**

Angels All Glorious

On the first Christmas, angels filled the midnight sky, singing gloriously of the birth of the Christ Child. The earth lay below — hushed in awe at the sight. "Peace on earth, good will to men" is a message that transcends the ages.

Listen ... can you hear the singing?

Christmas Tree Angel

Finished Size: 3¼" x 4"
46 x 56 Stitches

SYMBOL		COLOR	DMC	ANCHOR
▨	—	PINK	776	74
▵▵	—	DK. PINK	899	76
▲▲	—	RED	326	42
◿◹	—	PALE PEACH	754	778
		YELLOW	725	306
		DK. GREEN	561	212
▨	—	LT. BLUE	828	158
▵▲	—	NAVY BLUE	311	150
▵▵	—	BEIGE	842	933
		DK. BEIGE	841	378
▨	—	DK. BROWN	839	936
◿◹	—	BALGER® JAPAN GOLD #5		

NOTE: The colors without symbols are not used for Cross-stitch; they are used for details only.

FABRIC: This ornament was stitched on 14 count white perforated paper. A 4" x 5" piece is needed. For stitching, hold the paper so the long sides run vertically.

CROSS-STITCH: Use three strands of cotton floss. Use two strands of Japan Gold.

DETAILS: Use the number of strands indicated in parentheses.

Thin blue lines — 561 (2) Backstitch
Thick blue line — 725 (2) Straight Stitch
Thin pink lines — 326 (2) Backstitch
Thick pink lines — 839 (1) Backstitch
Thin black lines — 841 (2) Backstitch
Thick black lines — Japan Gold (2) Backstitch and Straight Stitch

The dotted lines indicate the cutting lines for finishing.

FINISHING: Our model was assembled using method #7, Perforated Paper (see page 159). The hanger and bow were made with 1⁄16" gold metallic cord.

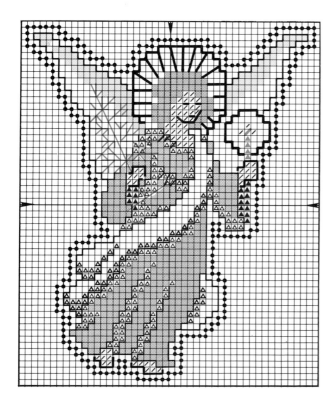

Garland Angel

Finished Size: 3¼" x 4"
45 x 58 Stitches

SYMBOL	COLOR	DMC	ANCHOR
△△	PINK	776	74
▲▲	DK. PINK	335	76
╱╱	PALE PEACH	754	778
	BRIGHT YELLOW	725	306
▦	GOLDEN BROWN	780	310
△△	DK. GREEN	561	212
╱╱	PALE BLUE	828	158
╱╱	LT. BLUE	3325	159
▲△	BLUE	334	161
▲▲	NAVY BLUE	311	150
△△	PURPLE	210	108
▦	BEIGE	842	933
	DK. BEIGE	841	378
	DK. BROWN	839	936
	BALGER® JAPAN GOLD #5		

NOTE: The colors without symbols are not used for Cross-stitch; they are used for details only.

FABRIC: This ornament was stitched on 14 count white perforated paper. A 4" x 5" piece is needed. For stitching, hold the paper so the long sides run vertically.

CROSS-STITCH: Use three strands to stitch.

DETAILS: Use the number of strands indicated in parentheses.

Thin pink lines — 839 (1) Backstitch
Thin blue lines — 311 (2) Backstitch
Thin black lines — 841 (2) Backstitch
Thick black lines — Japan Gold (2) Backstitch and Straight Stitch
Pink stars — 725 (2) French Knots

The dotted lines indicate the cutting lines for finishing.

FINISHING: Our model was assembled using method #7, Perforated Paper (see page 159). The hanger and bow were made with 1/16" gold metallic cord.

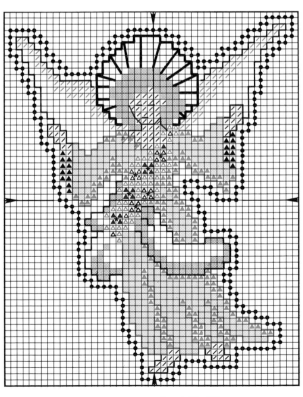

Angels All Glorious   **87**

Banner Angel

Finished Size: 4½" x 3"
65 x 45 Stitches

SYMBOL	COLOR	DMC	ANCHOR
△△ —	PINK	776	74
	DK. PINK	335	76
	CRANBERRY	326	42
▦ —	PALE PEACH	754	778
▲▲ —	RUST	921	339
—	PALE GREEN	369	260
△△ —	LT. GREEN	368	261
▲▲ —	DK. GREEN	561	212
△△ —	PALE BLUE	828	158
	LT. BROWN	841	378
	DK. BROWN	839	936
	BALGER® JAPAN GOLD #5		

NOTE: The colors without symbols are not used for Cross-stitch; they are used for details only.

FABRIC: This ornament was stitched on 14 count white perforated paper. A 5" x 4" piece is needed. For stitching, hold the paper so the long sides run horizontally.

CROSS-STITCH: Use three strands to stitch.

DETAILS: Use the number of strands indicated in parentheses.

Thin pink lines — 335 (2) Backstitch
Lettering — 326 (2) Backstitch
Thin blue lines — 561 (2) Backstitch
Thin black lines — 839 (1) Backstitch
Thick black lines — 841 (2) Backstitch
Thick blue lines — Japan Gold (2) Backstitch and Straight Stitch

The dotted lines indicate the cutting lines for finishing.

FINISHING: Our model was assembled using method #7, Perforated Paper (see page 159). The hanger and bow were made with ¹⁄₁₆" gold metallic cord.

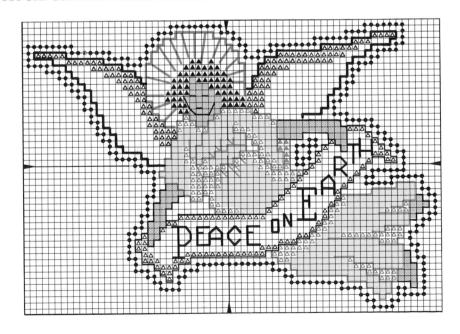

Peace Angel

Finished Size: 2½" x 3¼"
33 x 43 Stitches

SYMBOL	COLOR	DMC	ANCHOR
	RED	666	9046
△△ —	PALE PEACH	754	778
▲▲ —	PEACH	352	9
—	GOLD	977	308
—	PALE GREEN	369	259
△△ —	GREEN	368	261
▲▲ —	DK. GREEN	367	246
	DK. BLUE	312	162
▒ —	CREAM	712	275
▲▲ —	TAN	738	942
	DK. BROWN	3031	360
	BALGER® JAPAN GOLD #5		

NOTE: The colors without symbols are not used for Cross-stitch; they are used for details only.

FABRIC: This ornament was stitched on Wichelt Imports 18 count jonquil yellow Aida, color #105. A 5" x 6" piece is needed. For stitching, hold the fabric so the long sides run vertically.

CROSS-STITCH: Use two strands to stitch.

DETAILS: Use the number of strands indicated in parentheses.

Thin blue lines — 312 (2) Backstitch
Lettering — 666 (2) Backstitch
Pink hearts — 666 (2) French Knots
Thin black lines — 3031 (1) Backstitch and
    Straight Stitch
Black heart — 3031 (2) French Knot
Thick black lines — Japan Gold (1) Backstitch

FINISHING: Our model was assembled using method #1, Cardboard Cut-Out (see page 156). The edges were trimmed with ¹⁄₁₆" gold metallic cord and ¾" lace. The same gold metallic cord was also used to make the hanger. The bow was made of ⅛" satin ribbon.

Joy Angel

Finished Size: 2½" x 3¼"
36 x 47 Stitches

SYMBOL	COLOR	DMC	ANCHOR
⊡ —	Pink	776	74
◺◹ —	Dk. Pink	899	76
	Red	666	9046
⊠ —	Pale peach	754	778
◸◸ —	Gold	977	308
▦ —	Dk. Green	367	246
—	Dk. Blue	312	162
◹◹ —	Dk. Tan	402	369
⊞ —	Lt. Rust	922	338
▲▲ —	Rust	920	340
	Dk. Brown	3031	360
	Balger® Japan Gold #5		

NOTE: The colors without symbols are not used for Cross-stitch; they are used for details only.

FABRIC: This ornament was stitched on Wichelt Imports 18 count honeysuckle pink Aida, color #102. A 5" x 6" piece is needed. For stitching, hold the fabric so the long sides run vertically.

CROSS-STITCH: Use two strands to stitch.

DETAILS: Use the number of strands indicated in parentheses.

Thin blue lines — Japan Gold (1) Backstitch
Thick blue lines — 312 (2) Backstitch
Lettering — 666 (2) Backstitch
Pink stars — 666 (2) French Knots
Thin black lines — 3031 (1) Backstitch and
   Straight Stitch
Pink hearts — 3031 (2) French Knots

FINISHING: Our model was assembled using method #1, Cardboard Cut-Out (see page 156). The edges were trimmed with ¾" lace and ¹⁄₁₆" gold metallic cord. The same gold metallic cord was also used to make the hanger. The bow was made of ⅛" satin ribbon.

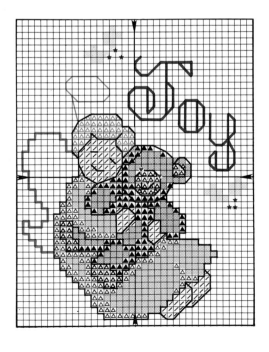

Love Angel

Finished Size: 3¼" x 2½"
42 x 36 Stitches

SYMBOL	COLOR	DMC	ANCHOR
	Red	666	9046
▲▲ —	Pale Peach	754	778
▦ —	Gold	977	308
▲▲ —	Dk. Green	367	210
▲ —	Lt. Blue	3325	159
▲ —	Blue	334	161
—	Dk. Blue	312	164
▦ —	Cream	712	275
▲▲ —	Tan	738	942
▲▲ —	Dk. Brown	3031	360
	Balger® Japan Gold #5		

NOTE: The colors without symbols are not used for Cross-stitch; they are used for details only.

FABRIC: This ornament was stitched on Wichelt Imports 18 count forget-me-not blue Aida, color #103. A 6" x 5" piece is needed. For stitching, hold the fabric so the long sides run horizontally.

CROSS-STITCH: Use two strands to stitch.

DETAILS: Use the number of strands indicated in parentheses.

Thin blue lines — 312 (2) Backstitch
Thin black lines — 3031 (1) Backstitch and
    Straight Stitch
Thin pink lines — 666 (2) Backstitch
Pink hearts — 666 (2) French Knots
Thick black lines — Japan Gold (1) Backstitch

FINISHING: Our model was assembled using method #1, Cardboard Cut-Out (see page 156). The edges were trimmed with ¹⁄₁₆" gold metallic cord and ¾" lace. The same gold metallic cord was also used to make the hanger. The bow was made of ⅛" satin ribbon.

Angel of the Year

Finished Size: 2" x 4"
22 x 49 Stitches

SYMBOL	COLOR	DMC	ANCHOR
△△ —	PINK	761	24
▲▲ —	RED	347	39
—	PALE PEACH	754	778
△△ —	BRIGHT YELLOW	725	306
—	LT. GREEN	504	213
△△ —	DK. GREEN	501	218
△△ —	TAN	739	933
—	DK. BROWN	3031	360
—	WHITE	White	1
▲▲ —	BALGER® JAPAN GOLD #5		

NOTE: The color without a symbol is not used for Cross-stitch; it is used for details only.

FABRIC: This ornament was stitched on Zweigart 14 count rue-green Aida, color #733. A 5" x 6" piece is needed. For stitching, hold the fabric so the long sides run vertically.

CROSS-STITCH: Use three strands of cotton floss. Use one strand of Japan Gold.

DETAILS: Use the number of strands indicated in parentheses.

    Thin pink lines — Japan Gold (1) Backstitch
    Thin black lines — 3031 (1) Backstitch
    Blue loops — 725 (2) Lazy Daisies
    Pink hearts — 347 (2) French Knots
    Date — 347 (2) Backstitch: Use the numbers from
       Personalizing Chart #3 (see page 154).

FINISHING: Our model was assembled using method #1, Cardboard Cut-Out (see page 156). The edges were trimmed with ¾" crocheted lace. Satin ribbon ⅛" wide was woven through the lace and used to make the bow and hanger.

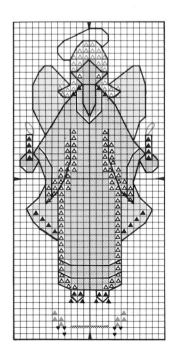

93

Stained Glass Angel

Finished Size: 2¼" x 4¾"
33 x 62 Stitches

SYMBOL		COLOR	DMC	ANCHOR
	—	PEACH	353	8
	—	ORANGE YELLOW	742	303
	—	BLUE	996	433
	—	BRIGHT BLUE	995	410
	—	NAVY BLUE	311	150
	—	LT. BROWN	301	351
	—	BALGER® JAPAN GOLD #5		

FABRIC: This ornament was stitched on Zweigart 18 count ivory Aida, color #264. A 5" x 9" piece is needed. For stitching, hold the fabric so the long sides run vertically.

CROSS-STITCH: Use two strands of cotton floss. Use one strand of Japan Gold.

DETAILS: Use the number of strands indicated in parentheses.

Wing outlines — 311 (1) Backstitch

FINISHING: Our model was assembled with painted wood hardware using method #2, Bellpull Banner (see page 157). The Monk's Cording was made with twelve strands of DMC #311. The tassel was also made with DMC #311.

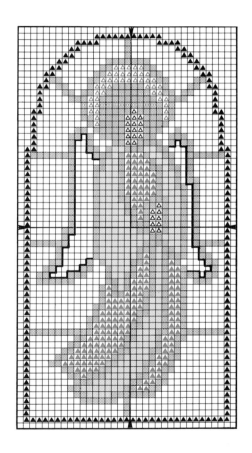

Face of an Angel

Finished Size: 3½" x 2½"
45 x 26 Stitches

SYMBOL		COLOR	DMC	ANCHOR
▵▵	—	ROSE	760	895
	—	DK. ROSE	3328	896
+ +	—	PALE PEACH	754	778
+ +	—	BRIGHT YELLOW	725	306
▵▵	—	LT. BLUE	827	159
	—	GREEN	987	245
	—	LT. RUST	402	369
		DK. BROWN	938	380

NOTE: The color without a symbol is not used for Cross-stitch; it is used for details only.

FABRIC: This ornament was stitched on Zweigart 18 count ivory Aida, color #264. A 6" x 5" piece is needed. For stitching, hold the fabric so the long sides run horizontally.

CROSS-STITCH: Use two strands to stitch.

DETAILS: Use the number of strands indicated in parentheses.

Thin blue lines — 987 (2) Straight Stitch
Thin black lines — 938 (1) Backstitch and
    Straight Stitch

FINISHING: Our model was assembled using method #9, Ready-Made Frame (see page 159). It was trimmed with ⅛" satin cording. The bow and hanger were made with ⅛" satin ribbon.

Folk Angel

Finished Size: 2" x 3"
33 x 50 Stitches

SYMBOL		COLOR	DMC	ANCHOR
	—	ROSE	760	895
	—	DK. ROSE	3328	896
	—	RED	347	39
	—	PALE PEACH	754	778
	—	YELLOW	725	306
	—	GREEN	987	245
	—	DK. BLUE	312	164
	—	TAN	738	942
	—	LT. BROWN	433	358
	—	DK. BROWN	938	380

NOTE: The color without a symbol is not used for Cross-stitch; it is used for details only.

FABRIC: This ornament was stitched on Zweigart 18 count ivory Aida. A 4" x 5" piece is needed. For stitching, hold the fabric so the long sides run vertically.

CROSS-STITCH: Use two strands to stitch.

DETAILS: Use the number of strands indicated in parentheses.

    Lettering — 987 (2) Backstitch
    Thin black lines — 938 (1) Backstitch
    Black hearts — 938 (2) French Knots

FINISHING: Our model was assembled using method #9, Ready-Made Frame (see page 159). The bow was made with ⅜" satin ribbon. Fine gold metallic cord was used for the trim and the hanger.

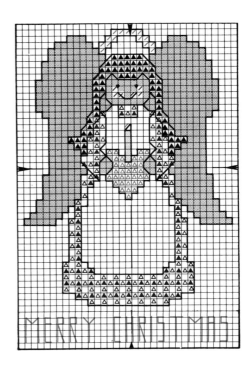

Through the Eyes of a Child

The wide-eyed wonderment of a child at Christmas evokes feelings of joy for us all. Holiday traditions of cookies and candy, jingle bells and trains, and Santa and his helpers are things most children wish they could celebrate all year long! By the way, a child wonders as he peeks up the fireplace, How does Santa fit into the chimney?

Georgie Gingerbread

Finished Size: 3" x 3½"
41 x 47 Stitches

SYMBOL	COLOR	DMC	ANCHOR
—	PINK	776	73
—	RED	321	47
	YELLOW	743	297
—	GREEN	699	923
—	BLACK	310	403
—	WHITE	White	1

NOTE: The color without a symbol is not used for Cross-stitch; it is used for details only.

FABRIC: This ornament was stitched on 14 count brown perforated paper. A 4" x 4" piece is needed.

CROSS-STITCH: Use three strands to stitch.

DETAILS: Use the number of strands indicated in parentheses.

Sweater outlines — 310 (1) Backstitch
Mouth — 310 (2) Backstitch
Nose — 310 (3) French Knots
Sweater buttons — White (3) French Knots
Hair — 743 (3) French Knots

The dotted lines indicate the cutting lines for finishing.

FINISHING: Our model was assembled using method #7, Perforated Paper (see page 159). The edges were covered with Monk's Cording made with eighteen strands of white. The hanger was made with ⅛" satin ribbon.

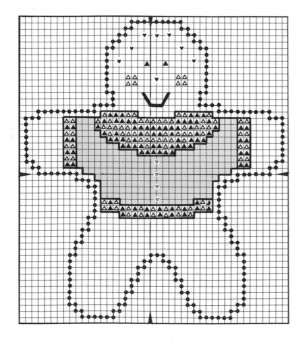

Peppermint Photo Frame

Finished Size: 3" Round
44 x 44 Stitches

SYMBOL	COLOR	DMC	ANCHOR
△△ —	PINK	893	27
▦ —	RED	321	9046
	GREEN	699	923

NOTE: The color without a symbol is not used for Cross-stitch; it is used for details only.

FABRIC: This ornament was stitched on 14 count white perforated paper. A 4" x 4" piece is needed.

CROSS-STITCH: Use three strands to stitch.

DETAILS: Use the number of strands indicated in parentheses.

Black lines — 321 (2) Backstitch
Blue lines — 699 (2) Backstitch
Date — 699 (2) Backstitch: Use the numbers from
  Personalizing Chart #10 (see page 155).

The dotted lines indicate the cutting lines for finishing.

FINISHING: Our model was assembled using method #8, Photo Frame (see page 159). The hanger was made with ⅜" satin ribbon.

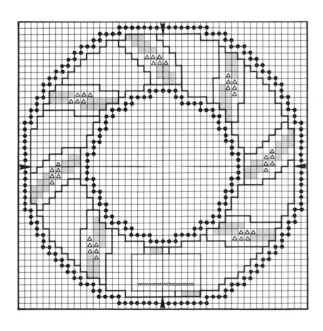

Crayon Christmas

Finished Size: 4" x 3"
38 x 23 Stitches

SYMBOL		COLOR	DMC	ANCHOR
	—	PINK	603	62
	—	RED	666	46
	—	ORANGE	970	316
	—	GREEN	700	228
	—	BLUE	996	433
	—	PURPLE	552	101
		BLACK	310	403

NOTE: The color without a symbol is not used for Cross-stitch; it is used for details only.

FABRIC: This ornament was stitched on Zweigart 11 count white Aida, color #1. A 6" x 5" piece is needed. For stitching, hold the fabric so the long sides run horizontally.

CROSS-STITCH: Use three strands to stitch.

DETAILS: Use the number of strands indicated in parentheses.

Name — 310 (3) Backstitch: Use the letters from Personalizing Chart #2 (see page154).
"Christmas" — 310 (3) Backstitch
Crayon outlines and letters:
  Purple crayon — 552 (3) Backstitch
  Green crayon — 700 (3) Backstitch
  Blue crayon — 996 (3) Backstitch
  Pink crayon — 603 (3) Backstitch
  Orange crayon — 970 (3) Backstitch

FINISHING: Our model was assembled using method #1, Cardboard Cut-Out (see page 156). The hanger was made of white rattail, threaded with four ⅜" plastic heart beads. Three 1" plastic crayon beads were threaded on 1/16" satin ribbon to dangle below the ornament.

Candy Stripe Stocking

Finished Size: 3" x 4"
42 x 55 Stitches

SYMBOL	COLOR		DMC	ANCHOR
▲▲ —	RED		321	47
	YELLOW		743	297
▦ —	GREEN		912	205

NOTE: The color without a symbol is not used for Cross-stitch; it is used for details only.

FABRIC: This ornament was stitched on Zweigart 14 count white Aida, color #1. A 5" x 6" piece is needed. For stitching, hold the fabric so the long sides run vertically.

CROSS-STITCH: Use three strands to stitch.

DETAILS: Use the number of strands indicated in parentheses.

> Name — 321 (3) Backstitch: Use the letters from Personalizing Chart #9 (see page 155).
> Black hearts — 743 (3) French Knots
> Attach four ¼" jingle bells with 321 (2).

FINISHING: Our model was assembled using method #1, Cardboard Cut-Out (see page 156). The hanger was made with ¹⁄₁₆" satin ribbon.

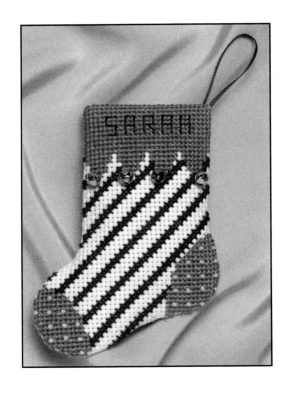

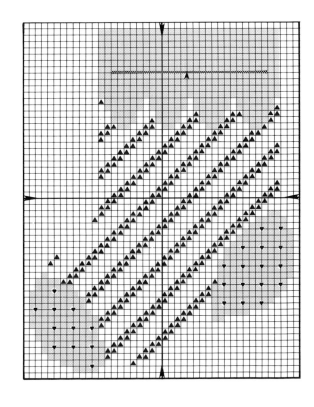

Major Mistletoe

Finished Size: 2¼" x 6¼"
23 x 56 Stitches

SYMBOL		COLOR	DMC	ANCHOR
J J	—	LT. PEACH	353	8
+ +	—	PINK	3708	26
▲▲	—	DK. RED	498	20
△△	—	YELLOW ORANGE	741	314
+ +	—	YELLOW	743	297
▲▲	—	GREEN	700	228
△△	—	LT. BLUE	809	130
	—	DK. BLUE	798	132
	—	BLACK	310	403
△△	—	WHITE	White	1

You may also need DMC 666. See FINISHING below.

FABRIC: This ornament was stitched on Wichelt Imports 14 count red Aida, color #954. A 5" x 11" piece is needed. For stitching, hold the fabric so the long sides run vertically.

CROSS-STITCH: Use three strands to stitch.

DETAILS: Use the number of strands indicated in parentheses.

    Black lines — 310 (1) Backstitch
    Nose — 310 (3) French Knot
    Pink lines — White (2) Straight Stitch
    Coat buttons — 741 (3) French Knots

FINISHING: Our model was assembled with white wood hardware using method #2, Bellpull Banner (see page 157). The hanger was made of two-color Monk's Cording, using twelve strands each of DMC #666 and white.

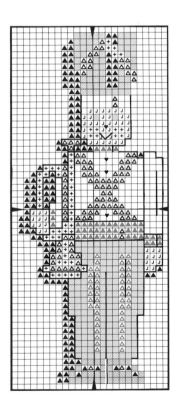

Uh-Oh! Santa

Finished Size: 2½" x 4"
28 x 50 Stitches

SYMBOL			COLOR	DMC	ANCHOR
+	+	—	PINK	776	24
△	△	—	LT. PEACH	353	8
▲	▲	—	YELLOW	743	297
▲	▲	—	GREEN	912	205
△	△	—	LT. GRAY	415	398
▲	▲	—	BLACK	310	403
		—	WHITE	White	1

FABRIC: This ornament was stitched on Wichelt Imports 14 count red Aida, color #954. A 5" x 6" piece is needed. For stitching, hold the fabric so the long sides run vertically.

CROSS-STITCH: Use three strands to stitch.

DETAILS: Use the number of strands indicated in parentheses.

Black lines — 310 (1) Backstitch
Eyes — 310 (2) French Knots
Pink lines — White (2) Backstitch and
    Straight Stitch
Pink heart — White (2) French Knot

FINISHING: Our model was assembled using method #1, Cardboard Cut-Out (see page 156). The edges were covered with ⅛" satin ribbon. The braided hanger and tassels were made with #3 white perle cotton. Six ¼" jingle bells were knotted at the ends of the tassels.

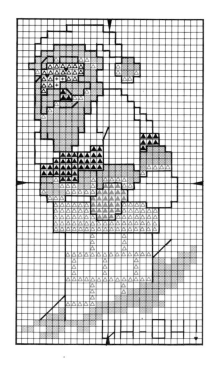

Rudolph

Finished Size: 3" x 3¾"
33 x 44 Stitches

SYMBOL		COLOR	DMC	ANCHOR
	—	RED	666	46
	—	YELLOW	743	297
	—	GREEN	700	228
	—	BRIGHT BLUE	996	433
	—	RUST	921	339
	—	BROWN	300	352
	—	BLACK	310	403

FABRIC: This ornament was stitched on Zweigart 14 count white Aida, color #1. A 5" x 6" piece is needed. For stitching, hold the fabric so the long sides run vertically.

CROSS-STITCH: Use three strands to stitch.

DETAILS: Use the number of strands indicated in parentheses.

Black lines — 300 (1) Backstitch
Pink lines — 310 (2) Backstitch
Blue lines — 700 (2) Backstitch and Straight Stitch
Date — 700 (2) Backstitch: Use the numbers from Personalizing Chart #11 (see page 155).
Attach a ¼" jingle bell to the bottom of the wreath with 743 (2).

FINISHING: Our model was assembled using method #1, Cardboard Cut-Out (see page 156). The hanger was made with ⅜" satin ribbon, and a ½" jingle bell was knotted at the top. It was trimmed with a ⅞" satin ribbon tail to which three ½" jingle bells were attached.

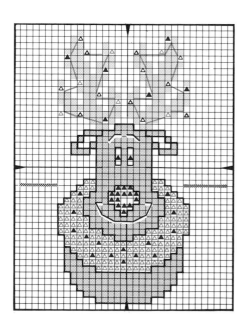

Christmas Express

Finished Size: 2½" x 6¼"
25 x 56 Stitches

SYMBOL		COLOR	DMC	ANCHOR
▲▲	—	RED	666	46
△△	—	YELLOW	743	297
⣿	—	ORANGE	741	304
△△	—	PALE GREEN	955	206
▲▲	—	BRIGHT BLUE	996	433
△△	—	LT. GRAY	3072	234
▲▲	—	BLACK	310	403
⣿	—	WHITE	White	1

FABRIC: This ornament was stitched on Zweigart 14 count green Aida, color #670. A 5" x 11" piece is needed. For stitching, hold the fabric so the long sides run vertically.

CROSS-STITCH: Use three strands to stitch.

DETAILS: Use the number of strands indicated in parentheses.

Black loops — white (2) Lazy Daisies
Black lines — 310 (1) Backstitch
Thick pink loops — 743 (2) Lazy Daisies
Thin pink loops — 666 (2) Lazy Daisies
Pink lines — 666 (2) Backstitch and
   Straight Stitch
Blue loops — 996 (2) Lazy Daisies
Blue hearts — 996 (3) French Knots

FINISHING: Our model was assembled with white wood hardware using method #2, Bellpull Banner (see page 157). The hanger was made with ⅛" satin ribbon.

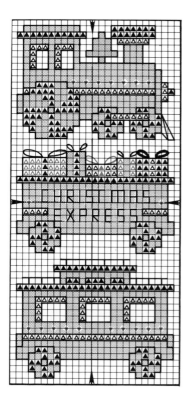

Skating Snowman

Finished Size: 3" x 4"
32 x 42 Stitches

SYMBOL		COLOR	DMC	ANCHOR
+ +	—	PINK	776	74
	—	RED	666	46
▲▲	—	ORANGE	947	330
△△	—	LT. YELLOW	744	301
△△	—	DK. YELLOW	742	303
	—	GREEN	703	238
+ +	—	LT. BLUE	800	159
△△	—	BRIGHT BLUE	996	433
+ +	—	LT. GRAY	3072	234
▲▲	—	BLACK	310	403
	—	WHITE	White	1

BALGER® JAPAN SILVER #5

NOTE: The color without a symbol is not used for Cross-stitch; it is used for details only. You may also need DMC 798. See FINISHING below.

FABRIC: This ornament was stitched on Zweigart 14 count blue Aida, color #540. A 5" x 6" piece is needed. For stitching, hold the fabric so the long sides run vertically.

CROSS-STITCH: Use three strands to stitch.

DETAILS: Use the number of strands indicated in parentheses.

Thin black lines — 310 (1) Backstitch
Thick black lines — Japan Silver (2) Backstitch
Blue lines — 800 (2) Straight Stitch

FINISHING: Our model was assembled using method #1, Cardboard Cut-Out (see page 156). The hanger and trim were made of two-color Monk's Cording, using twelve strands each of DMC #798 and white.

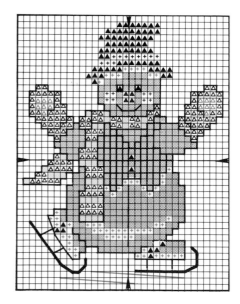

Laddie McMirth

Finished Size: 2" x 4"
27 x 55 Stitches

SYMBOL		COLOR	DMC	ANCHOR
	—	PINK	776	24
	—	YELLOW	743	297
	—	LT. GREEN	912	205
	—	DK. GREEN	699	230
	—	LT. RUST	977	363
	—	RUST	976	365
		BLACK	310	403
	—	WHITE	White	1
		GOLD BEADS (quantity, 2)		

NOTE: The color without a symbol is not used for Cross-stitch; it is used for details only.

FABRIC: This ornament was stitched on Wichelt Imports 18 count red Aida, color #954. A 4" x 6" piece is needed. For stitching, hold the fabric so the long sides run vertically.

CROSS-STITCH: Use two strands to stitch.

DETAILS: Use the number of strands indicated in parentheses.

> Black lines — 310 (1) Backstitch
> Eyes — 310 (2) French Knots
> Stocking stripes — White (2) Straight Stitch
> Tips of shoes — gold beads attached with 977 (2)

FINISHING: Our model was assembled using method #1, Cardboard Cut-Out (see page 156). The edges were trimmed with Monk's Cording, made with twenty-four strands of white. The hanger and bow were made of ¹⁄₁₆" satin ribbon. Two 1" wood candy canes were added to the ends of the bow.

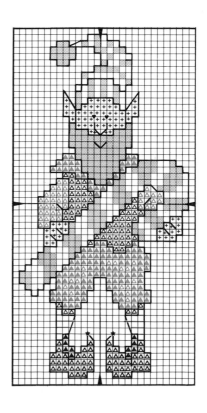

111

AMERICAN FLYER
640

290

A Critter's Christmas

Whether they're frolicking in the winter air or helping with holiday preparations, playful animals are an important part of Christmas. What better job for a giraffe than putting the star atop the tree? You know the puppy will be the best gift of all.

Sweet Treat Mouse

Finished Size: 2½" x 4¼"
35 x 51 Stitches

SYMBOL		COLOR	DMC	ANCHOR
▦	—	LT. PINK	761	894
▪▪	—	RED	666	46
x x	—	YELLOW	743	305
░	—	GREEN	911	230
▪▪	—	BLUE	517	162
░	—	LT. TAUPE	644	391
x x	—	TAUPE	642	392
		BLACK	310	403

NOTE: *The color without a symbol is not used for Cross-stitch; it is used for details only. You may also need white. See FINISHING below.*

FABRIC: This ornament was stitched on Zweigart 14 count white Aida, color #1. A 5" x 7" piece is needed. For stitching, hold the fabric so the long sides run vertically.

CROSS-STITCH: Use three strands to stitch.

DETAILS: Use the number of strands indicated in parentheses.

Thin black lines — 310 (1) Backstitch
Eyes and nose — 310 (3) French Knots
Thick black lines around pom-pom — 517 (1) Backstitch
Remaining thick black lines — 517 (1) Straight Stitch
Blue lines — 911 (2) Backstitch
Pink lines — 666 (2) Backstitch
Pink stars — 666 (3) French Knots

FINISHING: Our model was assembled using method #1, Cardboard Cut-Out (see page 156). It was trimmed with two-color Monk's Cording made with twelve strands of DMC #666 and twelve strands of white. The hanger and streamer were made with 1" satin ribbon. The bow was made with ⅜" satin ribbon, then tied with 1/16" satin ribbon.

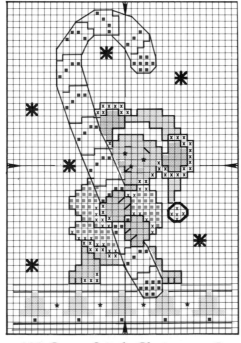

Can't Wait Kitten

Finished Size: 3" x 4"
31 x 50 Stitches

SYMBOL		COLOR	DMC	ANCHOR
	—	LT. PINK	761	894
	—	RED	666	46
		WINE	816	20
	—	YELLOW	743	305
	—	GREEN	911	230
	—	LT. TAUPE	644	391
	—	TAUPE	642	392
		BROWN	801	359
	—	BLACK	310	403

NOTE: The colors without symbols are not used for Cross-stitch; they are used for details only.

FABRIC: This ornament was stitched on Zweigart 14 count white Aida, color #1. A 5" x 6" piece is needed. For stitching, hold the fabric so the long sides run vertically.

CROSS-STITCH: Use three strands to stitch.

DETAILS: Use the number of strands indicated in parentheses.

   Thin blue lines — 801 (1) Backstitch
   Thick blue lines — 911 (1) Backstitch
   Thin pink lines — 816 (1) Backstitch
   Thick pink lines — 666 (1) Backstitch
   Thick black lines — 310 (2) Backstitch
   Thin black lines — 310 (1) Backstitch
   Black stars — 310 (3) French Knots

FINISHING: Our model was assembled using method #1, Cardboard Cut-Out (see page 156). The edges were trimmed with ⅜" piping. The hanger and bell strings were made of ¹⁄₁₆" satin ribbon. The bow was made of ⅜" satin ribbon. Three ½" bells were tied to the strings.

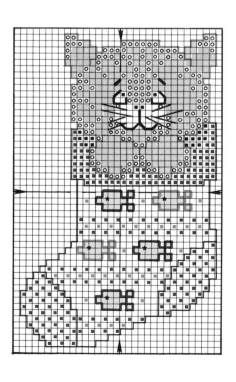

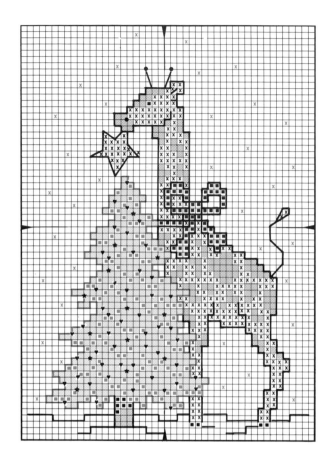

Star Bright Giraffe

Finished Size: 2½" x 4¼"
45 x 64 Stitches

SYMBOL		COLOR	DMC	ANCHOR
■■	—	RED	666	46
x x	—	PALE YELLOW	745	300
		YELLOW	743	305
▦	—	LT. GREEN	912	205
■▦	—	GREEN	699	923
x x	—	LT. TURQUOISE	598	167
		BLUE	996	433
▨	—	RUST	922	349
		DK. BROWN	898	360
■■	—	BLACK	310	403
		BALGER® GOLD #002		

BLENDED CROSS-STITCH — Two colors are threaded together in the needle to produce a lustrous effect.

x x	—	1 strand of 743; 1 strand of #002

NOTE: The colors without symbols are not used for Cross-stitch; they are used for Blended Cross-stitch or details only.

FABRIC: This ornament was stitched on Zweigart 18 count ivory Aida, color #264. A 5" x 7" piece is needed. For stitching, hold the fabric so the long sides run vertically.

CROSS-STITCH: Use two strands to stitch.

DETAILS: Use the number of strands indicated in parentheses.

Pink lines — 598 (2) Backstitch
Blue lines — 699 (1) Backstitch
Black lines — 898 (1) Backstitch
Nose — 898 (2) French Knot
Black hearts — 666 (2) French Knots
Black stars — 996 (2) French Knots
Pink hearts — 743 (1); #002 (1) French Knots

FINISHING: Our model was assembled using method #1, Cardboard Cut-Out (see page 156). It was trimmed with three ½" brass bells and a hanger made of ⅞" plaid ribbon. The hanger and bell strings were made of 1⁄16" satin ribbon.

Penguin Pair

Finished Size: 4" x 3½"
45 x 38 Stitches

SYMBOL	COLOR	DMC	ANCHOR
—	PINK	894	26
—	RED	666	46
—	YELLOW	743	305
—	GREEN	911	230
—	BLUE	996	433
—	BLACK	310	403

FABRIC: This ornament was stitched on Zweigart 14 count white Aida, color #1. A 6" x 6" piece is needed.

CROSS-STITCH: Use three strands to stitch.

DETAILS: Use the number of strands indicated in parentheses.

Date — 996 (2) Backstitch: Use the numbers from Personalizing Chart #7 (see page 155).
Blue lines — 996 (1) Straight Stitch
Pink lines — 666 (1) Backstitch
Black lines — 310 (1) Backstitch
Black stars — 310 (3) French Knots

FINISHING: Our model was assembled using method #1, Cardboard Cut-Out (see page 156). It was trimmed with a ¾" wide ruffle, then satin rattail. The bows and hanger were made of ¼" satin ribbon.

Polar Bear Pastime

Finished Size: 4¼" x 4¼"
48 x 48 Stitches

SYMBOL		COLOR	DMC	ANCHOR
x x	—	PINK	894	26
	—	RED	666	46
x x	—	YELLOW	743	305
	—	GREEN	911	230
		BLUE	996	433
x x	—	DK. BLUE	995	410
■ ■	—	BLACK	310	403

NOTE: The color without a symbol is not used for Cross-stitch; it is used for details only.

FABRIC: This ornament was stitched on Zweigart 14 count white Aida, color #1. A 7" x 7" piece is needed.

CROSS-STITCH: Use three strands to stitch.

DETAILS: Use the number of strands indicated in parentheses.

Date — 996 (2) Backstitch: Use the numbers from Personalizing Chart #3 (see page 154).
Pink lines — 996 (2) Straight Stitch
Blue lines — 995 (2) Backstitch
Thick black lines — 310 (2) Backstitch
Thin black lines — 310 (1) Backstitch
Black star — 310 (3) French Knot

FINISHING: Our model was assembled using method #1, Cardboard Cut-Out (see page 156). The board for the ornament back was cut ¼" larger than the front and covered with pindot calico. The hanger and bow were made of ¼" satin ribbon.

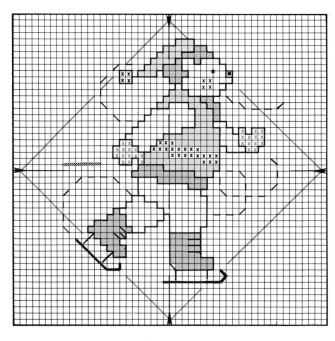

Christmas Cardinal

Finished Size: 4¼" x 4¼"
61 x 64 Stitches

SYMBOL		COLOR	DMC	ANCHOR
	—	ROSE	3328	38
x x	—	DK. ROSE	347	39
■ ■	—	RED	817	13
o o	—	LT. CORAL	350	11
o o	—	GOLD	977	363
x x	—	LT. GREEN	987	244
	—	GREEN	986	246
		LT. BLUE	334	977
x x	—	BROWN	975	355
■ ■	—	BLACK	310	403
	—	WHITE	WHITE	1

NOTE: The color without a symbol is not used for Cross-stitch; it is used for details only.

FABRIC: This ornament was stitched on Zweigart 18 count ivory Aida, color #264. A 7" x 7" piece is needed.

CROSS-STITCH: Use two strands to stitch.

DETAILS: Use the number of strands indicated in parentheses.

   Blue lines — 986 (1) Backstitch
   Pink lines — 334 (1) Backstitch
   Black lines — 310 (1) Backstitch
   Cardinal's eye — 310 (2)
     French Knot

FINISHING: Our model was assembled using method #1, Cardboard Cut-Out (see page 156). Plaid ribbon ⅞" wide was used to make the bow and the ⅛" piping trim. Satin ribbon 1/16" wide was used for the hanger and to attach a ½" bell to the bottom.

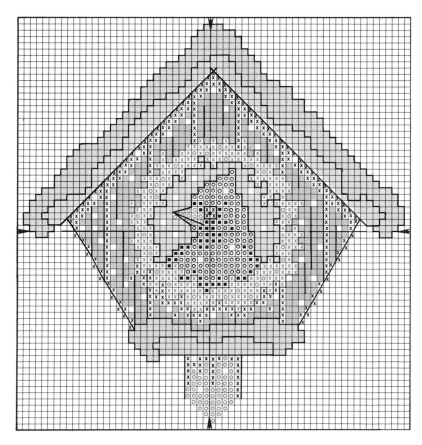

Precious Puppy

Finished Size: 3" Round
30 x 29 Stitches

SYMBOL		COLOR	DMC	ANCHOR
▨	—	RED	666	46
		WINE	816	20
X X	—	YELLOW	743	305
	—	LT. GREEN	912	205
▣	—	GREEN	699	923
X X	—	RUST	922	349
■ ■	—	DK. BROWN	938	380

NOTE: The color without a symbol is not used for Cross-stitch; it is used for details only.

FABRIC: This ornament was stitched on Zweigart 14 count ivory Aida, color #264. A 6" x 6" piece is needed.

CROSS-STITCH: Use three strands to stitch.

DETAILS: Use the number of strands indicated in parentheses.

Blue lines — 699 (1) Backstitch
Pink lines — 816 (1) Backstitch
Black lines — 938 (1) Backstitch

FINISHING: Our model was assembled using method #1, Cardboard Cut-Out (see page 156). It was trimmed with a ½" wide ruffle made of plaid ribbon. A ½" bell was sewn to the bottom of the ruffle. The hanger was made of ¹⁄₁₆" satin ribbon and the bow of ³⁄₈" satin ribbon.

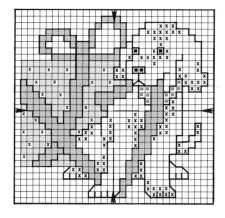

Loving Bunnies

Finished Size: 3" Round
36 x 38 Stitches

SYMBOL	COLOR	DMC	ANCHOR
xx	LT. PINK	761	894
■■	RED	666	46
oo	YELLOW	743	305
xx	LT. GREEN	912	205
	GREEN	909	230
oo	LT. BLUE	996	433
	BLUE	995	410
xx	GRAY	648	398
■■	BLACK	310	403

FABRIC: This ornament was stitched on Zweigart 14 count white Aida, color #1. A 5" x 5" piece is needed.

CROSS-STITCH: Use three strands to stitch.

DETAILS: Use the number of strands indicated in parentheses.

   Date — 995 (2) Backstitch: Use the numbers from Personalizing Chart #3 (see page 154).
   Black lines — 310 (1) Backstitch

FINISHING: Our model was assembled using method #1, Cardboard Cut-Out (see page 156). The board for the ornament back was cut ¼" larger than the front and covered with pindot calico. The hanger and bow were made of ¼" satin ribbon.

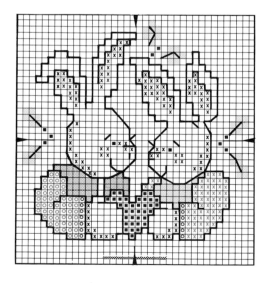

Holiday Lamb

Finished Size: 4" x 4"
38 x 38 Stitches

SYMBOL	COLOR	DMC	ANCHOR
▨ —	RED	349	13
	YELLOW	725	306
⊠ —	GREEN	909	230
▥ —	BLACK	310	403

NOTE: The color without a symbol is not used for Cross-stitch; it is used for details only.

FABRIC: This ornament was stitched on Zweigart 14 count ivory Aida, color #264. A 6" x 6" piece is needed.

CROSS-STITCH: Use three strands to stitch.

DETAILS: Use the number of strands indicated in parentheses.

Blue lines — 909 (2) Backstitch
Black lines — 310 (1) Backstitch
Pink hearts — 349 (3) French Knots
Pink lines — 725 (3) Backstitch
Black star — 725 (3) French Knot

FINISHING: Our model was assembled using method #4, Fringed Pillow (see page 158). The hanger was made of ⅜" satin ribbon.

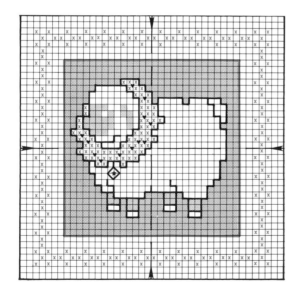

Holiday Duck

Finished Size: 4" x 4"
38 x 38 Stitches

SYMBOL	COLOR	DMC	ANCHOR
—	RED	349	13
—	YELLOW	725	306
—	GREEN	909	230
	BLACK	310	403

NOTE: The color without a symbol is not used for Cross-stitch; it is used for details only.

FABRIC: This ornament was stitched on Zweigart 14 count ivory Aida, color #264. A 6" x 6" piece is needed.

CROSS-STITCH: Use three strands to stitch.

DETAILS: Use the number of strands indicated in parentheses.

Pink lines — 349 (2) Backstitch
Black lines — 310 (1) Backstitch
Blue lines — 725 (2) Backstitch
Black star — 725 (2) French Knot

FINISHING: Our model was assembled using method #4, Fringed Pillow (see page 158). The hanger was made of ⅜" satin ribbon.

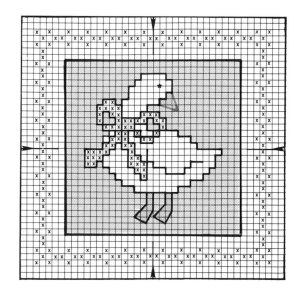

A Merrie Olde Christmas

Children caroling, shoppers laden with presents, holiday decorations, and seasonal greetings have all been part of holiday celebrations for hundreds of years. Joyful gatherings with family and friends return our spirits to those bygone days and rekindle warm, cozy memories of Christmas celebrations.

Olde English Noel

Finished Size: 2¼" x 5"
28 x 54 Stitches

SYMBOL	COLOR	DMC	ANCHOR
	RED	349	46
▦ —	GREEN	913	204
	BALGER® JAPAN GOLD #5		
	BALGER® RED CORD #003C		
▦ —	RED RIBBON ¹⁄₁₆" wide		

*NOTE: The colors without symbols are not used for
Cross-stitch; they are used for details only.*

FABRIC: This ornament was stitched on Charles Craft
14 count emerald-green Aida. A 5" x 9" piece is
needed. For stitching, hold the fabric so the long sides
run vertically.

CROSS-STITCH: Use three strands to stitch.

DETAILS: Use the number of strands indicated in
parentheses.

   Position the ribbon as shown by the gray shaded
     lines.
   Thick black lines — 349 (2) Straight Stitch
   Pink stars — 349 (3) French Knots
   Thin black lines — Japan Gold (2) Straight Stitch
   Pink lines — Red Cord (2) Backstitch

FINISHING: Our model was assembled with brass
bellpull hardware using method #2, Bellpull Banner
(see page 157). It was trimmed with a ½" jingle bell and
a ¹⁄₁₆" ribbon bow.

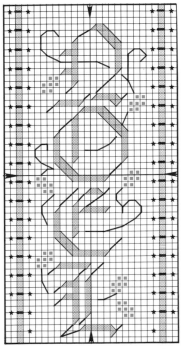

O' Tannenbaum

Finished Size: 3¾" x 3¼"
34 x 36 Stitches

SYMBOL		COLOR	DMC	ANCHOR
⊡⊡	—	CORAL	3705	35
		YELLOW	725	305
▦	—	LT. GREEN	564	206
✗✗	—	GREEN	562	211
■■	—	DK. BROWN	938	381
▨	—	WHITE	White	2
✗✗	—	BALGER® JAPAN GOLD #5		

NOTE: The color without a symbol is not used for Cross-stitch; it is used for details only.

FABRIC: This ornament was stitched on Charles Craft 14 count red Aida. Two 6" x 6" pieces are needed. One piece will be used to stitch the design and the second piece will be used for the background triangle.

CROSS-STITCH: Use three strands of cotton floss and two strands of Japan Gold.

DETAILS: Use the number of strands indicated in parentheses.

> Pink lines — 3705 (2) Straight Stitch
> Pink stars — 725 (2) French Knots
> Blue lines — Japan Gold (1) Backstitch
> Black lines — White (3) Straight Stitch

FINISHING: Our model was assembled using method #1, Cardboard Cut-Out (see page 156). The unstitched Aida was also mounted on a cardboard triangle shape. Both triangles were trimmed with ⅛" gold metallic cord. The triangle with the tree was attached to the front of the blank triangle. A ⅛" gold metallic cord hanger and a ½" jingle bell were added.

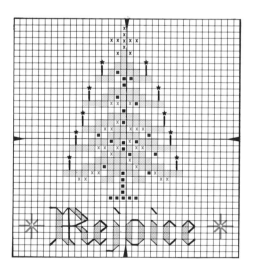

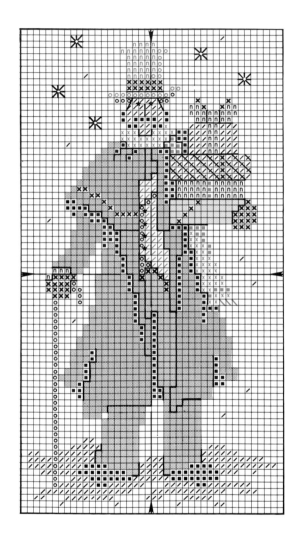

Last-Minute Shopper

Finished Size: 2¼" x 5½"
40 x 75 Stitches

SYMBOL	COLOR	DMC	ANCHOR
⁄⁄ —	Lt. Peach	353	8
n n —	Coral	3705	35
x x —	Dk. Red	817	47
■ ■ —	Lt. Rust	922	337
■ ■ —	Dk. Rust	919	341
⁄ ⁄ —	Gold	783	307
—	Lt. Green	564	206
x x —	Lt. Blue	827	159
■ ■ —	Bright Blue	826	161
n n —	Tan	738	361
o o —	Dk. Tan	436	365
o o —	Golden Brown	434	370
■ ■ —	Brown	898	360
—	Lt. Gray	452	232
x x —	Dk. Gray	413	401
—	Dk. Brown	3371	382
⁄ ⁄ —	White	White	1

NOTE: The color without a symbol is not used for Cross-stitch; it is used for details only.

FABRIC: This ornament was stitched on Zweigart 18 count navy Aida, color #589. A 5" x 10" piece is needed. For stitching, hold the fabric so the long sides run vertically.

CROSS-STITCH: Use two strands to stitch.

DETAILS: Use the number of strands indicated in parentheses.

Blue lines — 826 (1) Straight Stitch
Pink lines — 817 (1) Straight Stitch
Snowflakes — White (1) Backstitch
All remaining black lines — 3371 (1) Backstitch
Black stars — 3371 (2) French Knots

FINISHING: Our model was assembled with brass hardware using method #2, Bellpull Banner (see page 157). The sides were trimmed with ⅛" gold metallic cording. The bow was made of ⅜" satin ribbon.

CHARLES DICKENS

so much happiness. In the afternoon, he turned
nephew's house.

He passed the door a dozen times, before he ha
and knock. But he made a dash, and did it:

"Is your master at home, my dear?" said Scrooge

Very.
"Yes, sir."
"Where is he, my love?" said Scrooge.
"He's in the dining room, sir, along with mistr
upstairs, if you please."
He knows me," said Scrooge, with his ha
go in here, my dear."
and sidled his face in, round the
which was spread out in great
are always nervous on such point
ght.
oge.
how his niece by marriage starte
moment, about her sitting in the c
uldn't have done it, on any account.
soul!" cried Fred, "who's that?"
le Scrooge. I have come to dinner. W

s a mercy he didn't shake his arm off. He
Nothing could be heartier. His niece loo
pper when he came. So did the plump sis
eryone when they came. Wonderful party,
ul unanimity, won-der-ful happiness!
rly at the office next morning. Oh, he was ea
e there first, and catch Bob Cratchit coming
he had set his heart upon.
it; yes, he did! The clock struck nine. No Bob.
He was full eighteen minutes and a half behind
th his door wide open, that he might see him c

s off, before he opened the door; his comforter

102

Home for the Holidays

Finished Size: 2½" x 4¼"
34 x 51 Stitches

SYMBOL	COLOR	DMC	ANCHOR
	WINE	816	20
—	LT. RUST	922	337
×× —	RUST	921	339
∕∕ —	YELLOW	725	305
n n —	GREEN	992	187
—	TAN	739	276
—	DK. TAN	437	362
—	DK. BROWN	938	381
n n —	GRAY	452	232
×× —	BLACK	310	403
∕∕ —	WHITE	White	1

NOTE: The colors without symbols are not used for Cross-stitch; they are used for details only.

FABRIC: This ornament was stitched on Charles Craft 14 count emerald-green Aida. A 5" x 7" piece is needed. For stitching, hold the fabric so the long sides run vertically.

CROSS-STITCH: Use three strands to stitch.

DETAILS: Use the number of strands indicated in parentheses.

Name — White (2) Backstitch: Use the letters from Personalizing Chart #1 (see page 154).
Blue lines — 310 (1) Straight Stitch
Thin black lines — 938 (1) Backstitch
Bow on wreath — 816 (2): Use Lazy Daisies for the loops and Straight Stitch for the strings.

FINISHING: Our model was assembled using method #1, Cardboard Cut-Out (see page 156). It was trimmed with ⅛" satin cording. Using satin ribbons, a 1⅛" wide streamer, a ⅜" wide hanger, and a ⅝" wide bow were added.

Elegant Swan

Finished Size: 4" x 2"
50 x 24 Stitches

SYMBOL	COLOR	DMC	ANCHOR
	RED	321	47
⊙⊙ —	ORANGE	741	314
⁄⁄ —	LT. GREEN	563	208
⊙⊙ —	GREEN	562	211
⁄⁄ —	TAN	739	276
⁄⁄ —	DK. TAN	437	362
	DK. BROWN	3371	382
■■ —	BLACK	310	403
▦ —	WHITE	White	1
	BALGER® JAPAN GOLD #5		

NOTE: The colors without symbols are not used for Cross-stitch; they are used for details only.

FABRIC: This ornament was stitched on Charles Craft 14 count red Aida. A 6" x 4" piece is needed. For stitching, hold the fabric so the long sides run horizontally.

CROSS-STITCH: Use three strands to stitch.

DETAILS: Use the number of strands indicated in parentheses.

Blue lines — 562 (1) Backstitch
Black lines — 3371 (1) Backstitch
Black stars — White (3) French Knots
Bow — 321 (2): Use Lazy Daisies for the loops and Backstitch for the strings.
Remaining pink lines — Japan Gold (1) Backstitch
Pink stars — Japan Gold (1) French Knots

FINISHING: Our model was assembled using method #1, Cardboard Cut-Out (see page 156). The edges were trimmed with ⅛" gold metallic cord and ¼" satin cording. The hanger was also made of ⅛" gold metallic cord.

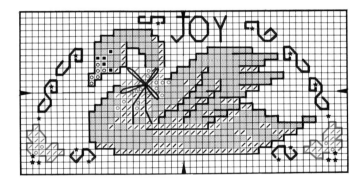

Luminous Lantern

Finished Size: 2" x 4"
31 x 65 Stitches

SYMBOL		COLOR	DMC	ANCHOR
	—	Lt. Red	350	11
	—	Dk. Red	817	13
	—	Orange	970	316
	—	Yellow	743	305
	—	Bright Green	911	230
	—	Lt. Gray	318	399
	—	Dk. Gray	317	400
		Dk. Brown	3371	382
	—	White	White	1

NOTE: The color without a symbol is not used for Cross-stitch; it is used for details only.

FABRIC: This ornament was stitched on Zweigart 18 count navy Aida, color #589. A 4" x 6" piece is needed. For stitching, hold the fabric so the long sides run vertically.

CROSS-STITCH: Use two strands to stitch.

DETAILS: Use the number of strands indicated in parentheses.

Pink lines — White (2) Backstitch
Blue lines — 318 (1) Backstitch
Black lines — 3371 (1) Backstitch

FINISHING: Our model was assembled using method #1, Cardboard Cut-Out (see page 156). The hanger and trim were made with ¼" satin cording and accented with heavy gold metallic thread at the bottom of the loop and the ends of the trim.

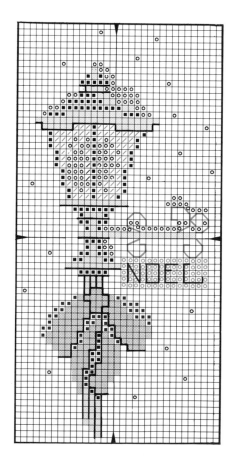

Santa's Sleigh

Finished Size: 4" x 3"
39 x 32 Stitches

SYMBOL	COLOR	DMC	ANCHOR
	RED	349	46
	DK. RED	817	47
	LT. CORAL	352	9
	GOLD	725	305
	LT. GREEN	563	208
	LT. BLUE	813	160
	BLUE	826	161
	LT. RUST	922	337
	DK. RUST	919	341
	DK. BROWN	938	381
	WHITE	White	1
	BALGER® CITRON #028		

BLENDED CROSS-STITCH — Two colors are threaded together in the needle to produce a lustrous effect.

— 2 strands of 725; 1 strand of #028

NOTE: The colors without symbols are not used for Cross-stitch; they are used for Blended Cross-stitch and details only.

FABRIC: This ornament was stitched on Charles Craft 14 count emerald-green Aida. A 6" x 5" piece is needed. For stitching, hold the fabric so the long sides run horizontally.

CROSS-STITCH: Use three strands to stitch.

DETAILS: Use the number of strands indicated in parentheses.

Date — 349 (2) Backstitch: Use the numbers from Personalizing Chart #4 (see page 154).
Black lines — 938 (1) Backstitch
Black loop — 938 (1) Lazy Daisy
Pink lines — 817 (1) Backstitch
Pink loops — White (2) Lazy Daisies
Blue lines — 826 (1) Straight Stitch
Blue loops — 563 (2) Lazy Daisies

FINISHING: Our model was assembled using method #1, Cardboard Cut-Out (see page 156). The ornament was trimmed with ⅛" gold metallic cord and ⅛" satin cording. Gold metallic cord was also used for the hanger.

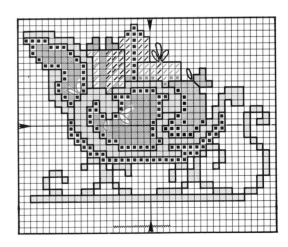

Skating Beauty

Finished Size: 3" x 4"
48 x 63 Stitches

SYMBOL		COLOR	DMC	ANCHOR
	—	LT. PEACH	353	8
	—	LT. RED	891	29
	—	GOLD	977	363
	—	LT. GREEN	563	208
	—	GREEN	562	211
	—	LT. BLUE	800	159
	—	BLUE	799	130
	—	DK. BLUE	798	132
	—	CREAM	712	926
	—	TAN	738	942
	—	BROWN	433	358
	—	DK. BROWN	898	360
	—	WHITE	White	1
		BALGER® JAPAN GOLD #5		

NOTE: The colors without symbols are not used for Cross-stitch; they are used for details only.

FABRIC: This ornament was stitched on Zweigart 18 count navy Aida, color #589. A 5" x 6" piece is needed. For stitching, hold the fabric so the long sides run vertically.

CROSS-STITCH: Use two strands to stitch.

DETAILS: Use the number of strands indicated in parentheses.

Thick blue lines — Japan Gold (1) Backstitch
Thin blue lines — 798 (1) Backstitch
Thick pink lines — 738 (2) Backstitch
Thick black lines — White (2) Backstitch
Thin black lines — 898 (1) Backstitch

FINISHING: Our model was assembled using method #1, Cardboard Cut-Out (see page 156). The bow and trim were made with ¼" satin cording and accented with heavy gold metallic thread at the center of the bow and at the bottom the ornament. The hanger was made from ⅛" gold metallic ribbon.

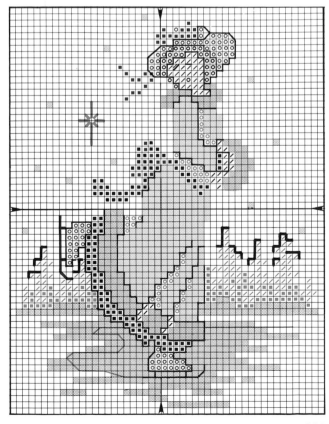

Carolers

Finished Size: 3¼" Round
52 x 52 Stitches

SYMBOL	COLOR	DMC	ANCHOR
⁄⁄ —	Lt. Peach	353	8
n n —	Lt. Red	349	13
▪ ▪ —	Dk. Red	817	47
X X —	Lt. Rust	922	347
—	Pale Yellow	745	300
x x —	Yellow	725	306
x x —	Lt. Green	564	206
X X —	Green	562	211
n n —	Lt. Blue	827	9159
▪ ▪ —	Bright Blue	826	161
—	Tan	738	942
⁄⁄ —	Golden Brown	436	943
▪ ▪ —	Brown	433	358
n n —	Gray	452	232
—	Dk. Brown	3371	382
▦ —	White	White	1

NOTE: The color without a symbol is not used for Cross-stitch; it is used for details only.

FABRIC: This ornament was stitched on Zweigart 18 count navy Aida, color #589. A 6" x 6" piece is needed.

CROSS-STITCH: Use two strands to stitch.

DETAILS: Use the number of strands indicated in parentheses.

Blue lines — 827 (2) Straight Stitch
Black lines — 3371 (1) Backstitch
Black stars — 3371 (2) French Knots

FINISHING: Our model was assembled using method #1, Cardboard Cut-Out (see page 156). The hanger was made of ⅛" gold metallic ribbon. The trim was made of ⅛" satin cording. Heavy gold metallic thread was used to accent the satin cording at the center of the bow and at the bottom of the ornament.

Holiday Horn

Finished Size: 3" Round
36 x 36 Stitches

SYMBOL	COLOR	DMC	ANCHOR
	PINK	894	26
	DK. PINK	892	28
	WINE	814	44
	PALE YELLOW	745	300
	YELLOW	725	305
	GOLD	976	308
	LT. GREEN	564	206
	GREEN	562	211
	DK. BROWN	938	381

NOTE: The colors without symbols are not used for Cross-stitch; they are used for details only.

FABRIC: This ornament was stitched on Charles Craft 14 count red Aida. A 5" x 5" piece is needed.

CROSS-STITCH: Use three strands to stitch.

DETAILS: Use the number of strands indicated in parentheses.

Blue lines — 562 (1) Backstitch
Thick pink lines — 892 (2) Backstitch
Thin pink lines — 814 (1) Backstitch
Black lines — 938 (1) Backstitch

FINISHING: Our model was assembled using method #1, Cardboard Cut-Out (see page 156). The edges were trimmed with ⅛" gold metallic cord, then ¼" satin cording. Satin cording was also used for the hanger and accented with heavy gold metallic thread at the ends.

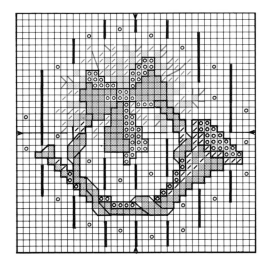

Yuletide Samplers

The timeless appeal of samplers couldn't be stronger than at Christmas. A simple theme and a cherished verse combine with delicate borders to express a holiday mood. Playful or joyful, a yuletide sampler strikes a pleasant chord in the hearts of everyone.

Vision of Santa

Finished Size: 2¾" x 5"
33 x 50 Stitches

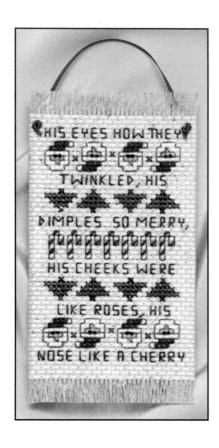

SYMBOL		COLOR	DMC	ANCHOR
	—	PEACH	353	8
	—	RED	321	9046
	—	GREEN	909	230
		BLUE	797	139
	—	DK. BROWN	801	359
	—	WHITE	White	1
		BLACK	310	403

NOTE: The colors without symbols are not used for Cross-stitch; they are used for details only.

FABRIC: This ornament was stitched on Zweigart 14 count oatmeal Rustico, color #54. A 5" x 7" piece is needed. For stitching, hold the fabric with the long sides running vertically.

CROSS-STITCH: Use three strands to stitch.

DETAILS: Use the number of strands indicated in parentheses.

    Pink lines — 321 (3) Straight Stitch
    Thick blue lines — White (3) Straight Stitch
    Thin blue lines — 797 (2) Backstitch
    Black lines — 801 (1) Backstitch
    Blue stars — 310 (2) French Knots

FINISHING: Our model was assembled using method #3, Fringed Banner (see page 158). The hanger was made of ¹⁄₁₆" satin ribbon.

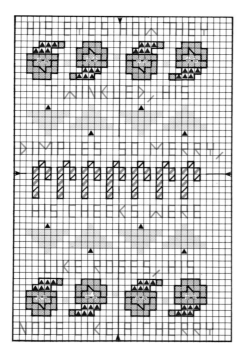

Let It Snow!

Finished Size: 2½" x 3½"
31 x 45 Stitches

SYMBOL		COLOR	DMC	ANCHOR
	—	RED	347	19
+	—	PALE YELLOW	745	300
	—	DK. GREEN	986	246
		LT. BLUE	775	975
△	—	DK. BLUE	311	148
▲	—	DK. BROWN	3031	360
△	—	GRAY	318	398
▲	—	BLACK	310	403
	—	WHITE	White	1

NOTE: The color without a symbol is not used for Cross-stitch; it is used for details only.

FABRIC: This ornament was stitched on Zweigart 14 count medium blue Aida, color #522. A 5" x 6" piece is needed. For stitching, hold the fabric with the long sides running vertically.

CROSS-STITCH: Use three strands to stitch.

DETAILS: Use the number of strands indicated in parentheses.

Thin pink lines — 347 (2) Backstitch
Thick pink lines — 3031 (2) Backstitch
Thick blue lines — 775 (2) Smyrna Cross-stitch
Thin blue lines — 311 (1) Backstitch
Verse lines — White (2) Backstitch
Verse dot — White (2) French Knot
Thin black lines — 310 (1) Backstitch
Black stars — 310 (2) French Knots

FINISHING: Our model was assembled using method #1, Cardboard Cut-Out (see page 156). The edges were trimmed with ⅛" piping and a ½" wide ruffle. The hanger and bow were made of ¼" satin ribbon.

Alphabet Heart

Finished Size: 4" x 3½"
70 x 56 Stitches

SYMBOL		COLOR	DMC	ANCHOR
△△	—	PINK	3326	75
	—	DK. PINK	335	57
▲▲	—	LT. GREEN	563	203
▦	—	GREEN	561	218
△△	—	CREAM	712	926

NOTE: The color without a symbol is not used for Cross-stitch; it is used for details only.

FABRIC: This ornament was stitched on Zweigart 18 count dk. red Aida, color #969. A 6" x 6" piece is needed.

CROSS-STITCH: Use two strands to stitch.

DETAILS: Use the number of strands indicated in parentheses.

Pink lines — 335 (2) Backstitch
Black lines — 561 (2) Straight Stitch

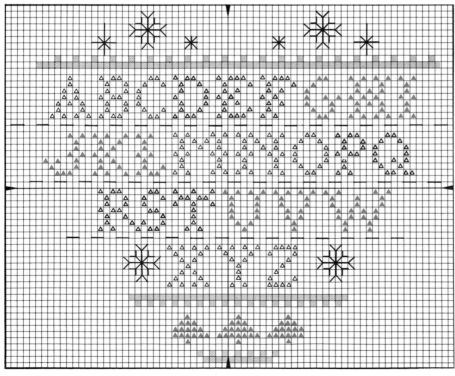

FINISHING: Our model was assembled using method #1, Cardboard Cut-Out (see page 156). It was trimmed with three rows of ⅛" piping. The hanger and bow were made of ¼" satin ribbons.

Country Cutter

Finished Size: 4" x 3½"
52 x 39 Stitches

SYMBOL	COLOR	DMC	ANCHOR
△△ —	PINK	760	894
—	RED	347	19
+|+ —	PALE YELLOW	745	300
△△ —	DUSTY GREEN	502	876
—	GREEN	561	218
△△ —	LT. BLUE	932	343
—	BLUE	930	922
▲▲ —	DK. BROWN	801	359

FABRIC: This ornament was stitched on Zweigart 14 count oatmeal Rustico, color #54. A 6" x 6" piece is needed.

CROSS-STITCH: Use three strands to stitch.

DETAILS: Use the number of strands indicated in parentheses.

    Blue lines — 561 (2) Backstitch
    Blue stars — 347 (3) French Knots
    Thin pink lines — 801 (1) Backstitch
    Thick pink lines — 801 (2) Backstitch
    Thick black lines — 932 (2) Straight Stitch
    Thin black lines — 930 (2) Backstitch

FINISHING: Our model was assembled using method #6, Cookie Cutter (see page 159). The edge of the cookie cutter was trimmed with ⅛" piping, then ¼" satin ribbon. The hanger and bows were also made of ¼" satin ribbon.

Celtic Christmas

Finished Size: 2½" x 5½"
34 x 75 Stitches

SYMBOL		COLOR	DMC	ANCHOR
▲▲	—	RED	321	9046
△▲	—	YELLOW	744	301
△△	—	GREEN	702	226
▲▲	—	DK. GREEN	699	923
		DK. BROWN	3031	360
▦	—	ECRU	Ecru	387

NOTE: The color without a symbol is not used for Cross-stitch; it is used for details only.

FABRIC: This ornament was stitched on Zweigart 32 count Belfast linen, color #23. A 5" x 10" piece is needed. For stitching, hold the fabric with the long edges running vertically.

CROSS-STITCH: Use two strands to stitch. Work each Cross-stitch over two fabric threads.

DETAILS: Use the number of strands indicated in parentheses.

Pink lines — 321 (2) Backstitch
Pink heart — 321 (2) French Knot
Blue lines — 744 (2) Backstitch
Pink stars — 321 (3) French Knots
Black lines — 3031 (1) Backstitch
Black stars — Ecru (3) French Knots

FINISHING: Our model was assembled with stained wood hardware using method #2, Bellpull Banner (see page 157). The Monk's Cording for the hanger was made with twelve strands of DMC #321. The tassel was also made with DMC #321.

O' Little Town

Finished Size: 3½" x 2½"
59 x 41 Stitches

FABRIC: This ornament was stitched on Zweigart 18 count summer khaki Aida, color #323. A 6" x 5" piece is needed. For stitching, hold the fabric with the long edges running horizontally.

CROSS-STITCH: Use two strands to stitch.

DETAILS: Use the number of strands indicated in parentheses.

> Thick blue lines — 3362 (2) Backstitch
> Thin blue lines — 3362 (1) Straight Stitch
> Thick pink lines — Japan Gold (1) Straight Stitch
> Thin pink lines — 938 (1) Backstitch
> Thick black lines — 712 (2) Backstitch
> Thin black lines — 930 (1) Backstitch

FINISHING: Our model was assembled using method #1, Cardboard Cut-Out (see page 156). The edges were trimmed with fine gold metallic cord and two rows of ⅛" piping. The hanger and bow were made of ⅛" satin ribbons.

SYMBOL	COLOR	DMC	ANCHOR
▲▲ —	CRANBERRY	816	43
△△ —	LT. OLIVE	3364	260
▲△ —	DK. OLIVE	3362	263
	BLUE	930	922
	DK. BROWN	938	380
	CREAM	712	926
	BALGER® JAPAN GOLD #5		

NOTE: The colors without symbols are not used for Cross-stitch; they are used for details only.

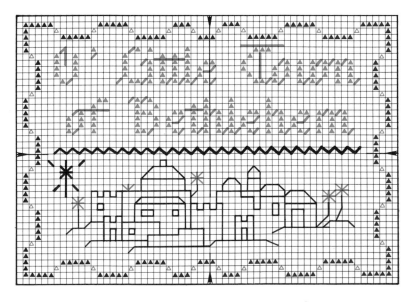

Adoration of the Magi

Finished Size: 3½" x 3"
59 x 43 Stitches

FABRIC: This ornament was stitched on Zweigart 18 count white damask Aida, color #1. A 6" x 7" piece is needed. For stitching, hold the fabric with the long sides running horizontally.

CROSS-STITCH: Use two strands to stitch.

DETAILS: Use the number of strands indicated in parentheses.

Thin black lines — 938 (1) Backstitch
Blue star — 938 (1) French Knot
Thick black lines — 336 (2) Backstitch
Black star — 336 (2) French Knot
Pink lines — Japan Gold (1) Backstitch
Pink star — Japan Gold (1)
    French Knot

FINISHING: Our model was assembled with stained wood hardware using method #2, Bellpull Banner (see page 157). The hanger was made of Monk's Cording, using two strands of Japan Gold.

SYMBOL		COLOR	DMC	ANCHOR
▲▲	—	CRANBERRY	498	43
▦	—	YELLOW	725	305
△△	—	GOLD	783	306
++	—	LT. OLD GOLD	781	309
△▲	—	OLD GOLD	780	310
△▲	—	GREEN	3346	268
▲	—	DK. GREEN	895	246
▦	—	DK. BLUE	336	150
▲▲	—	DK. PURPLE	550	102
	—	DK. BROWN	938	380
	BALGER® JAPAN GOLD #5			

NOTE: The colors without symbols are not used for Cross-stitch; they are used for details only.

Heavenly Host

Finished Size: 2½" x 4¼"
40 x 60 Stitches

SYMBOL	COLOR	DMC	ANCHOR
	PALE PEACH	754	4146
	WINE	816	43
	GOLD	729	890
	DK. GREEN	500	683
	DK. BROWN	938	380
	BALGER® JAPAN GOLD #5		

NOTE: The color without a symbol is not used for Cross-stitch; it is used for details only.

FABRIC: This ornament was stitched on Zweigart 18 count ivory damask Aida, color #264. A 5" x 9" piece is needed. For stitching, hold the fabric with the long sides running vertically.

CROSS-STITCH: Use two strands to stitch.

DETAILS: Use the number of strands indicated in parentheses.

> Date — 500 (2) Backstitch: Use the numbers from Personalizing Chart #3 (see page 154).
> Verse lines — 500 (2) Backstitch
> Verse dots — 500 (2) French Knots
> Black lines — 938 (1) Backstitch
> Star — Japan Gold (2) Smyrna Cross-stitch
> Remaining pink lines — Japan Gold (2) Backstitch

FINISHING: Our model was assembled with painted wood hardware using method #2, Bellpull Banner (see page 157). The hanger was made of ¹⁄₁₆" gold metallic cord.

Peaceful Poinsettias

Finished Size: 2½" x 3½"
44 x 63 Stitches

SYMBOL		COLOR	DMC	ANCHOR
	—	RED	817	47
	—	LT. OLIVE	3348	264
	—	GREEN	3345	268
	—	DK. GREEN	500	683
	—	BALGER® JAPAN GOLD #5		

FABRIC: This ornament was stitched on Zweigart 18 count white Aida, color #1. A 5" x 6" piece is needed. For stitching, hold the fabric with the long sides running vertically.

CROSS-STITCH: Use two strands to stitch.

DETAILS: Use the number of strands indicated in parentheses.

   Pink lines — Japan Gold (2) Backstitch
   Blue lines — 500 (1) Backstitch
   Black lines — 500 (2) Backstitch
   Black stars — 500 (2) French Knots

FINISHING: Our model was assembled using method #1, Cardboard Cut-Out (see page 156). The edges were trimmed with fine gold metallic cord, then ¼" satin cording. The hanger and bow were made of ⅛" satin ribbon.

Country Noel

Finished Size: 2½" x 5"
27 x 56 Stitches

SYMBOL		COLOR	DMC	ANCHOR
	—	RED	321	9046
	—	DK. RED	816	43
	—	YELLOW	743	305
	—	DK. GREEN	890	246

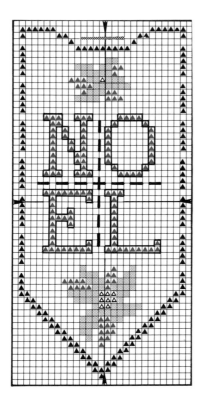

FABRIC: This ornament was stitched on Zweigart 25 count raw Dublin linen, color #53. A 5" x 9" piece is needed. For stitching, hold the fabric with the long sides running vertically.

CROSS-STITCH: Use three strands to stitch. Work each Cross-stitch over two fabric threads.

DETAILS: Use the number of strands indicated in parentheses.

Year — 890 (2) Backstitch: Use the numbers from Personalizing Chart #3 (see page 154).
Thick black lines — 816 (3) Straight Stitch
Thin black lines — 743 (1) Backstitch

FINISHING: Our model was assembled with stained wood hardware using method #2, Bellpull Banner (see page 157). The Monk's Cording for the hanger was made with twelve strands of DMC #890. The tassel was also made with DMC #890.

Personalizing Charts

These charts include the letters and numbers used on the ornaments. The directions for the personalized designs give the number of the appropriate personalizing chart you should use. To personalize your design, pencil the letters or numbers onto the gray line of the design chart before you begin working on the details.

Of course, any design can be personalized. For an heirloom touch, you may wish to personalize all of your handiworks with your initials and date. Charts #1 and #3 are a size that would fit almost anywhere.

If you don't wish to alter the appearance of the design, make the ornament back out of an even-weave fabric and put the personalizing there. If the ornament is a gift, the back is the perfect place for a special message such as:

To Tammy
With Love From Grandma
Christmas 1991

The blank graph paper is for your own experimentation. You may even consider making up your own letters and numbers, using ours as guides.

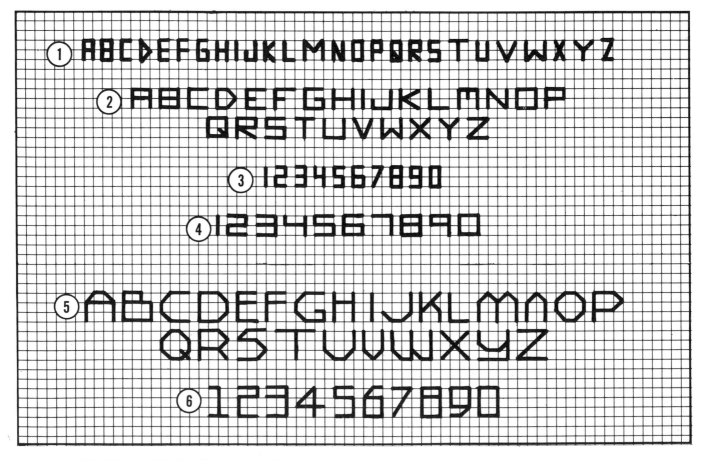

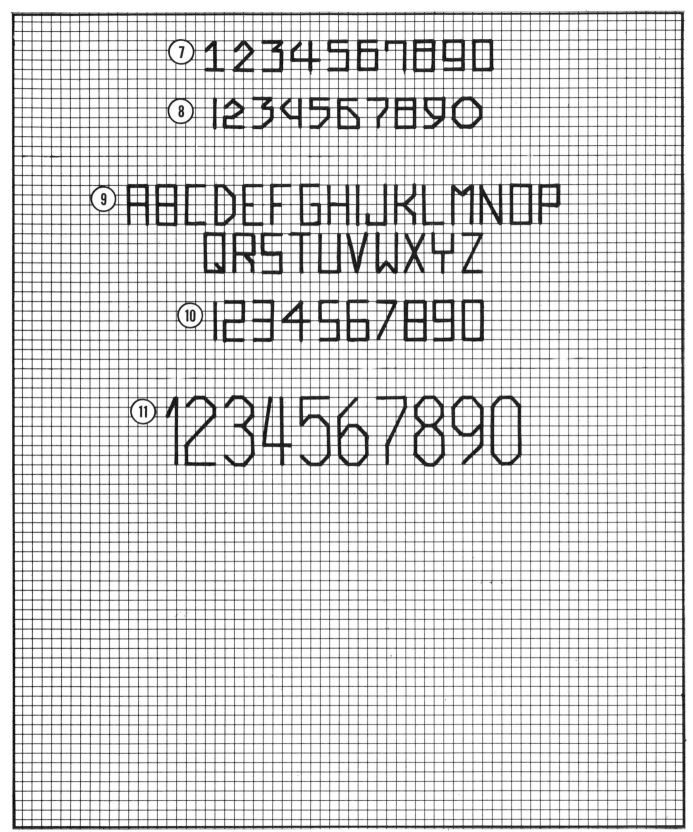

Finishings

Assembly Methods

Stitching your ornaments is fun, and finishing them can be just as creative and enjoyable! You can finish your ornaments as shown, or feel free to mix and match various assembly methods and trims. We have given you many sample ideas, but you can use your own imagination and ingenuity to create truly personal ornaments.

Before you purchase finishing materials, decide which method you wish to use. Any ornament can be finished in a variety of ways. It can be sewn together and stuffed like a little pillow, mounted on a cardboard cut-out and decorated, or made into a banner. We've included lots of ideas and instructions and they are all simple to do.

Once you've chosen your assembly method, you're ready to go out and buy trimming materials. Skim through the Ideas sections on pages 160 through 164 for inspiration. Start with your local hobby, craft and fabric stores, and take your ornaments with you! We carried our 100 ornaments along with us while we looked for materials, much to the delight of shop owners and clerks! Having your ornaments with you is essential in matching the colors and feel of the designs. You'll also be able to hold the materials next to your design to help you visualize the overall effect.

Look at our ornaments for inspiration, then take off in your own direction! Be fanciful and inventive. Remember, you're creating ornaments that your family and friends will treasure.

A few words about glue. Most of the assembly, edging, and trimming methods require the use of glue. We recommend using a thick craft glue or a hot glue gun. Both types of glue will bond almost anything and are quick to set up. White household glue is not recommended because it is messy and takes a good deal of time to dry.

#1 Cardboard Cut-Out

 This is a versatile method suitable for a variety of ornament shapes. Most of our ornaments were finished using this method. It gives your ornament a padded, ripple-free front with a smooth edge that's just waiting for an edging or trim! You can make the back in the same way or simply glue material to the back to hide the raw edges.

MATERIALS
- *Stiff cardboard for mounting board*
- *Quilt batting for padding*
- *Material for backing (fabric if adding a padded back; felt, wallpaper, or gift wrap if adding a flat back)*
- *Glue*
- *Tissue paper*

MOUNTING THE FRONT USING A PATTERN
Trace the appropriate pattern (see page 164) onto the tissue paper.

Use the tissue pattern to cut the mounting board from the cardboard and a layer of padding from the quilt batting. Use a dab of glue to attach the padding to the mounting board.

Center the tissue pattern on the design and pin it into place. Working ½" out from the edge of the pattern, cut out the design. Set the pattern aside for later use.

Center the design right side up over the padded side of the mounting board. Turn the excess fabric to the back of the mounting board. Notch or slit the excess fabric as shown so the fabric lies flat against the cardboard. Glue the fabric to the back of the cardboard.

Attach any lace, ruffles, or piping if desired, then add a hanger. See the sections on pages 160 through 163 for ideas and instructions.

MOUNTING THE FRONT WITH A FREE-FORM SHAPE
Baste the ornament outline around your design, using a contrasting thread. This is shown on the chart by the blue line. The dashes beside the line show where to break your basting stitches.

Lay the tissue paper over the design and trace the basting line to make a pattern. Use the pattern to cut the mounting board from the cardboard and a layer of padding from the batting. Use a dab of glue to attach the padding to the mounting board.

Cut out the design, working ½" out from the basting. Remove the basting.

Center the design right side up over the padding side of the mounting board. Turn the excess fabric to the back of the mounting board. Notch or slit the excess fabric as shown so the fabric lies flat against the cardboard. Glue the fabric to the back of the cardboard.

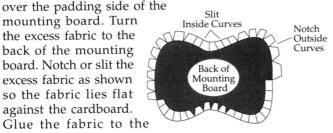

Slit Inside Curves

Notch Outside Curves

Back of Mounting Board

Attach any lace, ruffles, or piping if desired, then add a hanger. See the sections on pages 160 through 163 for ideas and instructions.

ADDING A PADDED BACK

Assemble the ornament back, using the same method as for the front. Glue the front and back together, holding the edges together until the glue has set.

ADDING A FLAT BACK

Trim ¼" from all sides of the pattern, then use it to cut out the backing material. Glue it to the back of the ornament.

#2 Bellpull Banner

This method is suitable for any long rectangular design. Small bellpull hardware is available at needlework and craft shops. If you can't find just the right look, make your own by gluing small beads to the ends of a dowel, then painting or staining them in a color that enhances your design.

The bottom of the banner can be plain, either square or pointed; it can be finished with hardware at the bottom; or it can be fringed.

MATERIALS
- *Small bellpull hardware (you'll need one or two depending on how you finish the bottom)*
- *Fabric for back*
- *Sewing thread*
- *Tissue paper*

FINISHING A BANNER WITH A PLAIN BOTTOM

Make a pattern on the tissue paper by drawing a rectangle the same size as the finished size. Add a ¼" seam allowance to the sides and bottom. Add 1¼" to the top. Position the pattern on the design so it is centered in the finished size rectangle. Cut out the design. Trim the end to a point if desired.

Use the pattern to cut out the back.

Place the front and back together, with the right sides facing and cut edges even. Sew them together, working ¼" from the cut edges around the sides and bottom. Leave the top edge open. Trim the seam allowance close to the stitching at the corners.

Turn the banner right side out and press the seams.

Turn both layers of the banner top ¼" to the wrong side and press. Place the hardware on the back and fold the top edge of the banner over it. Hand stitch the edge to the back, then add a hanger (see page 162).

Back of Banner

FINISHING A BANNER WITH A FRINGED BOTTOM

Make a pattern on the tissue paper by drawing a rectangle the same size as the finished size. Add a ¼" seam allowance to the sides. Add ½" to the bottom and 1¼" to the top. Position the pattern on the design so it is centered in the finished size rectangle. Cut out the design.

Use the front as a pattern to cut out the back. Turn the bottom edge ⅜" to the wrong side.

Place the front and back together, with the right sides facing and top edges even. Sew them together on the sides, working ¼" from the cut edges. Leave the top and bottom edges open.

Turn the banner right side out and press the seams.

Turn the top edge of the design ¼" to the wrong side and press. Place the hardware on the back and fold the top edge of the banner over it. Hand stitch the edge to the back.

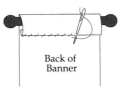

Back of Banner

Remove the horizontal fabric threads at the bottom to make ⅜" of fringe.

FINISHING WITH HARDWARE AT THE TOP AND THE BOTTOM

Make a pattern on the tissue paper by drawing a rectangle the same size as the finished size. Add a ¼" seam allowance to the sides. Add 1¼" to the bottom and to the top. Position the pattern on the design so it is centered in the finished size rectangle. Cut out the design.

Use the front as a pattern to cut out the back.

Place the front and back together with the right sides facing and top edges even. Sew them together on the sides, working ¼" from the cut edges. Leave the top and bottom edges open.

Turn the banner right side out and press the seams.

Turn the top edge of the design ¼" to the wrong side and press. Place the hardware on the back and fold the top edge of the banner over it. Hand stitch the edge to the back.

Back of Banner

Repeat to add the hardware at the bottom.

#3 Fringed Banner

This method is suitable for any long rectangular design. It is quick to do and gives the design an informal country touch.

MATERIALS
- *Felt for back*
- *Glue*
- *Tissue paper*

METHOD

Make a pattern on the tissue paper by drawing a rectangle the same size as the finished size. Add ½" to the width. Position the pattern on the design so it is centered. Cut out the design. Trim ⅝" from the width of the pattern and ¾" from the length. Use the pattern to cut the back from the felt.

On both sides of the design, press ¼" to the wrong side.

Center the felt back on the wrong side of the ornament and glue into place.

Remove ⅜" of horizontal fabric threads to fringe the top and bottom edges.

#4 Fringed Pillow

This method is suitable for square or rectangular designs. The fringe gives the ornament a rustic look.

MATERIALS
- *Fabric for ornament back*
- *Stuffing*
- *Sewing thread*
- *Tissue paper*

METHOD

Draw a square the same size as the finished size on a piece of tissue paper. Use this as a pattern to cut out the ornament front and back. Make sure the design is centered when cutting out the front.

Place the front and back together, with the *wrong* sides facing and cut edges even. Sew the front and back together, placing the stitches ½" in from the cut edges and leaving a 1½" opening at the center bottom.

Front of Design

Insert a small amount of stuffing into the pocket, then complete the stitching at the bottom.

Remove fabric threads to fringe the edges up to the stitching.

#5 Wrapped Frame

This method is suitable for any round design. The frame can be wrapped with calico for a country look or with a polished chintz or sateen for a more elegant look.

MATERIALS
- *Stiff cardboard for frame and mounting board*
- *Lightweight fabric for frame*
- *Yarn for padding*
- *Glue*

METHOD

Draw a circle on the cardboard the same size as the finished size. Draw another circle ⅜" larger, centering it around the first circle. Cut out both circles so that you have a ring for the frame and a solid circle for the mounting board.

Wrap the frame with the yarn, completely covering the cardboard.

Cut a strip from the fabric, which has a width of 1" and a length ten times the diameter of the mounting board. On one long edge, press ¼" of the fabric to the wrong side.

Wrap the yarn-covered frame with the fabric strip, pulling the fabric firmly as you work. Space the wraps evenly and as far apart as possible. Continue wrapping until you cover the first two starting wraps.

To end, trim the excess fabric and tuck the raw edge under the last wrap. Apply a dab of glue to keep the end in place.

Glue the design to the mounting board, making sure it is centered. Cut off the excess fabric ¼" outside the edge of the mounting board. Add a hanger to the frame, then glue the frame to the design.

#6 Cookie Cutter

 This method is suitable for any design around which a cookie cutter will fit. The cookie cutter gives a wonderful, old-fashioned warmth to the design.

MATERIALS
- *Metal cookie cutter without handle*
- *Cardboard for mounting board*
- *Quilt batting for padding*
- *Felt for backing*
- *Glue*
- *Tissue paper*

METHOD
Place the cookie cutter on the tissue paper and trace around the inside edge to make a pattern.

Use the pattern to cut the mounting board from the cardboard and a layer of padding from the quilt batting. Test the mounting board in the cookie cutter to make sure that it fits easily; there should be room for the fabric. Use a dab of glue to attach the padding to the mounting board.

Use the pattern to cut the back from the felt.

Center the pattern on the design and pin it in place. Working ¼" out from the edge of the pattern, cut out the design.

Center the design right side up over the padded side of the mounting board. Turn the excess fabric to the back of the mounting board. Notch or slit the excess fabric as shown so the fabric lies flat against the cardboard. Glue the fabric to the back of the cardboard.

Back of Mounting Board

Notch Outside Curves

Slit Inside Curves

Glue the felt backing to the back of the cardboard.

Insert the design into the cookie cutter. On the back, secure it with a few drops of glue where the fabric and cookie cutter meet.

#7 Perforated Paper

 Perforated paper is perfect for ornaments; the finishing couldn't be easier. Just cut out the design, add a hanger and backing, and your ornament is ready to go!

MATERIALS
- *Small, sharp-pointed scissors*
- *Paper for back*
- *Glue*

METHOD
Cut out the design, following the dotted lines on the chart.

Add a hanger to the design.

Using a very thin layer of glue, attach the design to the backing paper. Trim the backing paper, either next to the perforated paper or working ⅛" out from the edges.

#8 Photo Frame

 This method makes a wonderful personalized package tie-on or gift. It's a great way to send school photos to relatives and friends.

MATERIALS
- *Small, sharp-pointed scissors*
- *Paper for back*
- *Photo to fit opening*
- *Glue*

METHOD
Cut out the frame, following the dotted lines on the chart.

Center the frame on the photo. Trace the outer edge of the frame onto the photo. Cut out the photo, working ¼" in from the traced line.

Using a very thin layer of glue, attach the photo to the frame.

Add a hanger.

Again using a very thin layer of glue, attach the backing paper. Trim the backing paper to the same size as the frame.

#9 Ready-Made Frame

If you're pressed for time, there are many pre-made plastic or wooden frames designed just for ornaments. Or try using a small 3" embroidery hoop as a frame. These items can be used alone or along with other trims to dress them up. Either way, they're a fast and attractive alternative for Christmas Eve finishing!

Cording & Piping Ideas

Adding some type of cording or piping to the edge of your ornament brings out the colors in the design. It also helps to frame the design by giving it a finished edge. It's one of our favorite ways to begin trimming ornaments. The following are some materials we've found useful for this purpose:

Rattail — A smooth satiny cord.

Satin rope cording — Available in a variety of widths.

Perle cotton — A shiny cotton thread available in a variety of weights.

Metallic cord — Available in many widths in fabric and gift-wrap stores.

Monk's Cording — Can't find a pre-made cording in a color to match your design? Make your own, using embroidery floss or metallic thread.

Jute twine — Great for a primitive or country look.

Strings of beads — Try gold beads, pearls, and small glass beads.

Yarn — Use rug yarn or craft yarn.

Piping — Can be bought ready-made in packages or by the yard; or make your own using ribbon or fabrics.

Cording or piping can be used by themselves as the finishing touch or in combination with laces and ruffles. You can also use two rows of piping or cording, such as a thin inner one with a heavy outer one. They can be different colors, or one satin and one metallic. Choose whatever appeals to you!

Working with Cording

MEASURING

If you are using ready-made cording, you will need a piece equal to the perimeter of the ornament plus two inches.

If you are making Monk's Cording, you will have to determine how long and wide you want the finished cording to be. You will need to start with floss that is 2½ times as long as the finished piece of cording. Twelve strands will make cording about ⅛" wide. Use more or fewer strands to achieve the width you desire.

Whenever you cut either Monk's Cording or ready-made cording, knot the cut ends or wrap them with tape to prevent them from untwisting.

MAKING ONE COLOR MONK'S CORDING

Lay the strands of floss side by side. Have someone hold one end of the floss taut while you hold the other.

Twist the floss clockwise at both ends until it begins to curl on itself. Grab the floss at the middle and put the loose ends together. Release the middle and allow the floss to continue to twist.

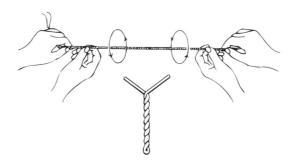

Adjust the twists so they look smooth and even. Knot the loose ends together to prevent them from untwisting.

MAKING TWO-COLOR MONK'S CORDING

Each of the two colors should be 1¼ times as long as the finished piece of cording. Knot the two colors of floss together at one end. Divide the floss so that one color is on one side of the knot and one color is on the other side. Have someone hold one end of the floss taut while you hold the other.

Twist the floss clockwise at both ends until it begins to curl on itself. Grab the knot at the middle and put the loose ends together. Release the knot and allow the floss to continue to twist.

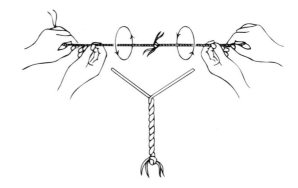

Adjust the twists so they look smooth and even. Knot the loose ends together to prevent them from untwisting.

ATTACHING CORDING AROUND THE EDGE

Apply a thin line of craft glue around the outside edge of the ornament. Press the cording into place on the line of glue.

Overlap the ends, then turn the extra cording to the back of the ornament.

If possible, choose a starting and stopping point that will not show when the ornament is finished — a position that will be hidden with a bow or other trim, for example. Trim off the extra cording if desired.

ATTACHING CORDING WITH A BOW AND TAILS

Make a loop in the center of the cording.

Pinch the loop in the center to form two bow loops. Wrap the loops at the center with ornamental floss to secure them.

Wrap Here First

Ornament Front

Wrap Here Next

Attach the bow to the top of the ornament. Attach the cording to the sides of the ornament, having the cording meet at the center bottom. Wrap the two pieces of cording together at the center bottom with ornamental thread. Trim the cording ends if desired.

ATTACHING CORDING WITH A LOOP

Make a loop in the center of the cording. Wrap the loop at the base with ornamental thread to secure.

Attach the base of the loop to the top of the ornament. Attach the cording to sides of the ornament, ending about halfway down the sides. Trim the cording to the desired length and wrap the ends with ornamental thread.

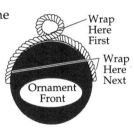

Wrap Here First

Wrap Here Next

Ornament Front

Working with Piping

MEASURING

If you are using ready-made piping, you will need a piece equal to the perimeter of the ornament plus two inches.

If you are making your own piping, you will need a piece of filler cord that is equal to the perimeter of the ornament plus two inches. You will also need a 12" square piece of fabric from which to cut the strips to cover the cord.

MAKING PIPING

Working on the bias (diagonally between two corners), cut fabric strips 1½" wide.

Lay the cord in the middle of the fabric strip and fold the fabric over it. Using a zipper foot, sew through both layers of fabric as close to the cord as possible.

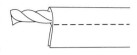

ATTACHING PIPING

Apply a thin line of glue to the ornament back, near the edge.

Position the piping on the ornament so it is visible on the front and the seam allowance is pressed into the glue on the back. If possible, choose a starting and stopping point that will not show when the ornament is finished — a position that will be hidden with a bow or other trim, for example.

Overlap the piping as smoothly as possible, turning the ends to the back of the ornament. Trim off the extra piping if desired.

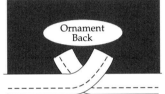

Ornament Back

Ruffle & Lace Ideas

With today's increased interest in home sewing and crafts, there is a gold mine of ready-made pregathered ruffles and laces. We've discovered printed pregathered fabric ruffles with or without a second layer of lace, prepleated satin ribbon, and prepleated taffeta ruffles. There are many varieties of flat and pregathered laces — from very delicate nylon laces to heavy crocheted-look laces. We've even found gold metallic lace, which we used on our Snowflake ornaments (see pages 52-55)!

If your search does not turn up just the right ready-made ruffle, you can always create your own. Any ribbon or fabric would make a terrific ruffle.

Need ideas for how to use your finds? Try just a single layer of gathered lace or a single fabric ruffle. How about an outer fabric ruffle with an inner layer of gathered lace? Or two layers of lace, different in width or color? Or two layers of ruffled fabric, different in width? Or a print and a solid? Get the idea?

Working with Lace

MEASURING

If you are using pregathered lace, you will need a piece equal to the perimeter of the ornament plus one inch.

If you are gathering your own lace, you should begin with a piece of flat lace that is two times as long as the perimeter of the ornament. This will give you a lace ruffle that is nice and full.

Gathering the Lace
Work a row of basting stitches ⅛" from the straight edge. Gather the lace until the length equals the length of the outside edge of the ornament plus one inch.

Adjust the gathers so they look smooth and even. Knot the thread ends so the gathers stay in place.

Attaching the Lace
Apply a thin line of glue to the ornament back, near the edge.

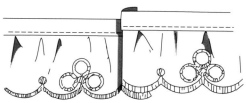

Press lace into place, onto the line of glue, overlapping the lace ends where they meet. If possible, choose a starting and stopping point that will not show when the ornament is finished — a position that will be hidden with a bow or other trim, for example. Trim off the extra lace if desired.

Working with Ruffles

Measuring
If you are using a pregathered ruffle, you will need a length equal to the perimeter of the ornament plus one inch.

If you are making your own ruffle from fabric, you will need a strip of fabric that is two times as long as the perimeter of the ornament. This will give you a ruffle that is nice and full. The fabric should be two times as wide as you want the finished ruffle to be plus one half inch.

If you are making your own ruffle from ribbon, you will need a piece of ribbon that is two times as long as the perimeter of the ornament.

Gathering the Ruffle
If you are using fabric, fold it in half lengthwise, with the wrong sides together. Work a row of basting stitches through *both* layers of fabric, ⅛" from the cut edge.

If you are using ribbon, work a row of basting stitches ⅛" from one straight edge.

Gather the ruffle until the length equals the perimeter of the ornament plus one inch.

Adjust the gathers so they look smooth and even. Secure the thread ends so the gathers stay in place.

Attaching the Ruffle
Apply a thin line of craft glue to the ornament back, near the edge.

Press the ruffle into place on the line of glue, overlapping the ruffle ends where they meet. If possible, choose a starting and stopping point that will not show when the ornament is finished — a position that will be hidden with a bow or other trim, for example. Trim the extra ruffle if desired.

Hanger & Bow Ideas
Hangers can be made from any material that coordinates with the other materials used in your ornament. The length of the hanger depends on whether you will use wire hooks to hang your ornaments or prefer to have a hanger large enough to go over the tree branch. In any case, hangers must be attached in a position that's centered on the ornament or the design will not hang properly.

Bows serve a practical function by hiding the starting and stopping point of your laces, ruffles, or cording. If you've looked at our ornaments and wondered why you don't see any seams, we'll tell you our secret — it's all in the placement of the bows!

Bows can be made from any material, from ribbon to twine to cording to fabric. They can be anything from two simple loops to ornate multiple loops with long or short tails. The bow can be placed at the top of the ornament with tails that fall behind it and extend below the bottom, or it can be positioned at the bottom of the ornament.

Try out the size of the loops by making a few and holding them next to your ornament. Adjust the size to achieve the desired effect. No matter what the color, material, or position, a bow is a beautiful addition to any ornament.

Making Hangers

MATERIALS
- *Hanger material*
- *Glue or thread to secure the loops*

Shown at right are several ways of folding the material to make a hanger. Glue the hanger to the back of the ornament before the backing is attached so the ends will be hidden. For extra security, you may wish to stitch the hanger to the back of the ornament.

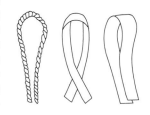

Making Bows

MATERIALS
- *Bow material*
- *Glue or thread*
- *Ribbon for covering center of bow*

TWO-LOOP BOW
Make two loops the same size as shown. Glue or stitch where the loops overlap.

You may wish to cut a short length of ribbon and wrap it around the center of the loops to cover the overlap. Glue the wrapped piece together at the back.

MULTILOOP BOW
Hold the bow material in one hand with the length between the thumb and the index finger. Put most of the length at the back and have the tail in front a little longer than the desired finished length. Using the long end, make a loop above your fingers and hold it tightly. Make the second loop below your fingers.

Repeat, making as many loops as desired.

Hold the loops together in the center. Tie a piece of thread tightly around the center to secure the loops.

Cut a short length of ribbon, and wrap it around the center of the loops to cover the thread. Glue the wrapped piece together at the back.

TAILORED BOW
This type of bow works best with ribbon that is at least 1" wide.

Cut a piece of ribbon to the desired length. Make a circle by overlapping the ends ½". Glue or stitch the ends together.

Press the center top of the loop to the bottom, making two loops of equal size. Glue or stitch the two loops into place.

Cut a short length of ribbon to make a single loop. Wrap the loop around the center and glue or stitch it to the back of the bow.

Trim & Tassel Ideas

Often it's the little extras you find that give an ornament the final touch of beauty or panache. Listed below are some starting ideas for material possibilities.

Flowers — Silk ribbon roses, small silk flowers, beaded flowers used in bridal crafting, sprigs of silk evergreens or holly, dried flowers, baby's breath.

Wooden shapes — Small hearts painted to match your design, or prepainted shapes such as teddy bears, Santas, hearts, etc.

Doll house miniatures — Small candy canes or Santas, for example. Our little crayons on the Crayon Christmas ornament (see page 102) fall into this category. There are so many cute, tiny items available for doll houses that would be great for dressing up your ornaments.

Wreaths — Grapevine, straw, or other dried or silk materials in a wreath shape can be used to frame your ornaments. Just mount the design onto cardboard of an appropriate size and glue it to the wreath.

Tassels — You can buy these premade or you can make your own. The ones we used on the Turn-of-the-Century Elegance ornaments (see pages 42-55) were cut from tassel fringe used for upholstery. The other tassels were made by us. They're easy to do, and have the advantage of being exactly the right color to match your ornament, since they're made with the same floss.

Baubles and doo-dads — Jingle bells; small cow bells; beads made of glass, wood or plastic; sequins; stars.

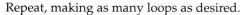

Attaching Trims

Attaching the trims is done in one of two ways: they can be tacked on with a few stitches, or they can be glued. The method you choose is up to you — whatever works best for that particular item. If at all possible, however, bells should be stitched on so they can jingle.

Making Tassels

MATERIALS
- *Cotton or rayon embroidery floss*
- *Sewing needle*

Our tassels were made with between 30 and 40 pieces of six-strand floss. However, by adjusting the size and number of lengths you use, your tassel can be whatever size you desire.

Cut floss lengths twice as long as you want the finished size of your tassel to be. Lay all lengths side by side with cut ends even. Take an additional piece of the same-color floss and tie the lengths together at the center with a knot. Fold the floss in half at the tie.

Thread a needle with a six-strand 18" length of the same-color floss. Move the needle to the center of the length, then tie the loose ends together with a knot. Working ½" from the fold, loop the floss around the tassel, then pass the needle through the loop.

Hold the knot so the ends point toward the tassel fold. Working toward the tassel fold and rotating the tassel toward the left, *tightly* wrap the floss over the knot and around the tassel. Continue to wrap the tassel for about ¼". If properly wrapped, the knot will not show. If the knot does show, unwrap and begin again.

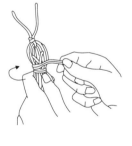

Holding the wraps tightly, insert the needle at the top of the wraps, then pull the needle down through the center of the tassel. Cut out the needle, then tie the loose ends together in a knot at the center of the tassel. Trim the ends of the tassel so they are even.

Attach the tassel to the ornament with a few stitches.

Patterns

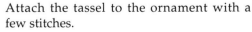

Choosing the right pattern can help add that special look to your ornament. While some of our designs are made to fit a specific shape, others lend themselves to a variety of shapes. Choose the shape that suits both the stitched design and you!

Trace the pattern onto a piece of tissue or tracing paper. This piece of paper can then be centered over the embroidery and the design cut out. If you would like your patterns to be more permanent, try making them out of heavier paper or cardboard.

A
Rudolph

B
Stained Glass Joy

C
Stained Glass Candles
Stained Glass Dove

D
Christmas Cardinal
Jean Claude Bearly
Polar Bear Pastime
Snowflake Diamond

E
Uh-Oh! Santa

F
Let It Snow!
O' Little Town
Peaceful Poinsettias

G
Patchwork Mitten

H
Beary Best Friends
O' Tannenbaum
Santa Bear

I
Candy Stripe Stocking
Can't Wait Kitten
Crazy Quilt Stocking
Stocking Bear

J
Patchwork Stocking

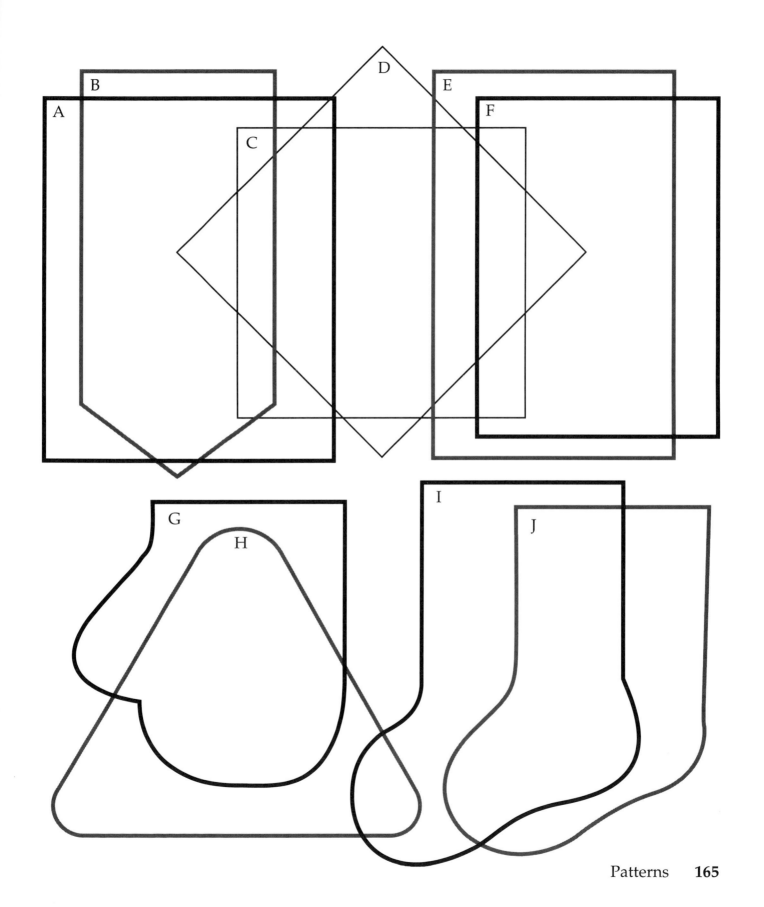

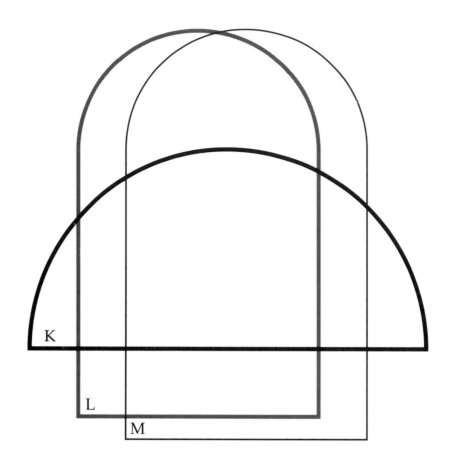

K
Crazy Quilt Fan
Elegant Swan
Rosebud Fan

L
True Blue Santa

M
Christmas Chapel
Home for the Holidays
Star Bright Giraffe
Sweet Treat Mouse
The Holy Family
Waiting for Santa

N
Rosebud Heart

O
Alphabet Heart
Folk Heart
Penguin Pair

P
Crazy Quilt Heart

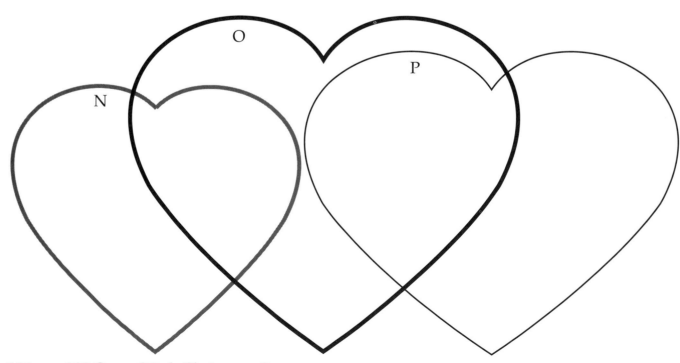

Q

Gilded Noel
Glittering Snowflake
Holiday Horn
Loving Bunnies
Père Noel
Precious Puppy
Sparkling Snowflake

R

Rosebud Circle

S

Christmas Goose
My Friend Sally
Pull Toy Sheep

T

Carolers

U

Angel of the Year
Baby New Year
Folk Art Angel
Holiday Steed
Laddie McMirth
Luminous Lantern
Mountain Santa

V

Manger Scene
Crayon Christmas
Father Christmas
Gifts of the Magi
Joyful Tidings Bear
Legendary Santa
Madonna and Child
Santa's Sleigh
Skating Beauty
Skating Snowman
The Herald Angel

W

Flame-stitch Rosebuds
Joy Angel
Love Angel
Peace Angel

X

Candlelit Scripture

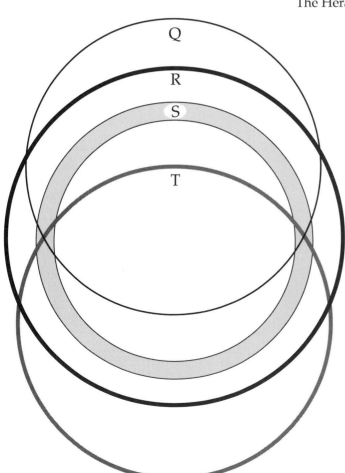

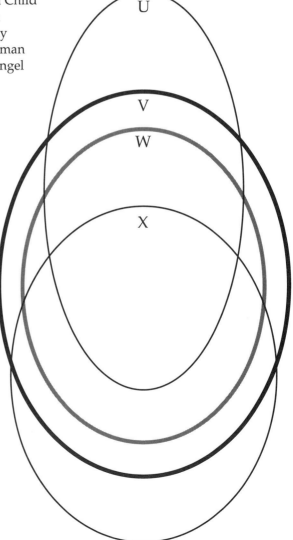

Index